DAY HIKES
& OVERNIGHTS
ON THE
PACIFIC CREST TRAIL

SOUTHERN CALIFORNIA

DAY HIKES & OVERNIGHTS
ON THE
PACIFIC CREST TRAIL

SOUTHERN CALIFORNIA

From the Mexican Border
to Los Angeles County

Marlise Kast-Myers

THE COUNTRYMAN PRESS
WOODSTOCK, VERMONT

Cover design by Benjamin Myers
Maps by Erin Greb Cartography, © The Countryman Press
Book design and composition by Susan Livingston
Interior photographs by Marlise Kast-Myers, Rory Lavender,
or Justin McChesney-Wachs, as noted

Published by The Countryman Press, P.O. Box 748, Woodstock, VT 05091
Distributed by W. W. Norton & Company, Inc., 500 Fifth Avenue, New York, NY 10110
Printed in the United States of America

Day Hikes & Overnights on the Pacific Crest Trail, Southern California
978-1-58157-202-5

10 9 8 7 6 5 4 3 2 1

Dedicated to the Creator of all things beautiful.

Acknowledgments

To my hiking partner, Claire: Thank you for joining me on this rewarding journey. Your passion for the great outdoors has been an inspiration every step of the way. Ben, thank you for your guidance and direction, both on the trail and in my life. Mom, thank you for encouraging me to combine my love for writing and fitness into one unforgettable experience. Dad, thank you for instilling in me a desire to climb every mountain, even those that may appear too steep. Finally, Heidi, my sister, thank you for teaching me how to tie my shoes. Who would have guessed that such a basic skill could take me so far?

Contents

Preface

| Views of Cottonwood Canyon below

As a San Diego local who has circled the globe, I was pleased to discover the stunning beauty of the Pacific Crest Trail (PCT) virtually in my own backyard. Over a prolonged series of weekend getaways, I had the privilege of hiking more than 400 miles of that magnificent trail.

When I look back at my first hike, I remember the way my calves cursed me for not having given them time to fully prepare for what loomed ahead. Despite the pain the following day (or was it days?), I wholeheartedly challenged myself to endure another 44 hikes for the sake of reaching my goal.

Admittedly, as a travel writer, I often blur the line between work and play. In this case, my office became the trail, rush hour morphed into the passing of a jackrabbit, and office memos consisted of GPS waypoints and map coordinates. Despite the welcome abnormality of this project, I was determined to quickly finish the task, check it off my bucket list, and move on to yet another unwritten book sitting on my mental shelf.

An interesting thing happened along the way, however: The Pacific Crest Trail and I started to become friends. Sometime around the third or fourth hike, I began to see the PCT as a living, breathing entity. Whether I liked it or not, we were going to get to know one another extremely well.

There were times when the PCT and I did not see eye-to-eye, especially during the scorching, 23-mile wasteland journey across the Anza-Borrego Desert. Elsewhere in that section, as I paused beside the tiered cascades of the trail's waterfalls, I realized there was no place I would rather be.

Just as one gets to know a friend, I came to appreciate the unique characteristics of the PCT. Trees became recognizable by sight, flowers by scent, and birds by sound. Our friendship blossomed in early May, when buttercups and poppies tilted their fragile petals toward the sun. The air smelled of sage and honey. Even in the heart of the desert, the trail was pleasantly splashed with creamy, white yucca buds and cactus flowers broadcasting shades of fuchsia and lime from thorny pads.

Winter magically transformed the trail into a blanket of whiteness, punctuated by trees heavily laden with fresh snow. Each backward glance at the solitary imprint of my snow-shoes reminded me of the peace and solitude one can find on the PCT. Intoxicated by nature, I macro-photographed everything, from butterflies and lizards to branches and petals. Seldom could I pass a shrub or plant without snapping another picture. The PCT was no longer a goal, but rather a road of discovery.

It is my desire that you too will experience the southern portion of the PCT in all its splendor, from the steel walls of Mexico to the desolate valleys of the Angeles National Forest. Although it's rugged in the beginning, you will discover that the trail visually softens as it leaves the Mexican border and drops into emerald valleys and trickling streams.

The greatest points of reference, however, have nothing to do with flora, fauna, trailheads, or creek crossings. They have to do with the memories birthed on the trail of enriching conversations on tedious switchbacks, mental photographs snapped at sunset, and compassionate locals who offered advice along the way.

Despite photographs, journal entries, and the tread left behind, what endures most is the solid imprint the PCT leaves on our souls. Fortunately, that alone is enough to keep me at peace for years to come. I hope this will also be your experience as you embark on your own journey into the wild.

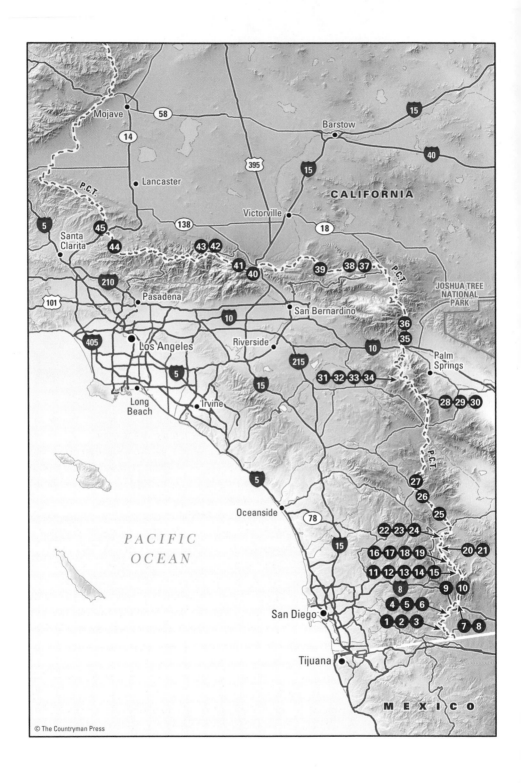

Introduction

About This Book

In choosing these hikes, my goal was to cater to everyone from the day hiker in search of a comfortable loop to the committed Pacific Crest Trail (PCT) warrior who slows down only at sunset. The majority of these trails are easily accessible from anywhere in the greater San Diego or Los Angeles areas.

Thirty-four of the hikes, ranging from one to twelve miles, can be enjoyed as day hikes. I've mentioned appealing camping spots, which are particularly useful for anyone wanting to link to the next featured trek. The remaining 11 routes, ranging from 12 miles to 46 miles, appeal to hikers who prefer to extend nature's pleasures with overnight experiences or longer distances. For those hikes, I've noted camping facilities or areas that invite an overnight experience. This guide includes trail distances in the Table of Contents and at the beginning of each section.

Stretching from Mexico to Canada, the 2,650-mile PCT (250 miles of which run through private land) is traversed by more than 350 thru-hikers annually. In addition, thousands of day hikers drop on and off the famed trail, officially designated by Congress on October 2, 1968. Rising from desert lowlands to snowcapped mountains, the PCT passes through six North American eco-zones, offering diversity and transformation along the way.

For many, the highlight of the PCT is the 650-mile stretch running through Southern California. The southernmost section, starting at the Mexican border, is often maligned because of the chaparral landscape, dry terrain, and scorching summer heat. This lackluster commencement, however, makes one truly appreciate what lies ahead.

A steep climb out of Hauser Canyon leads to Lake Morena County Park, where shoreline campsites are a family favorite. This welcome departure from scrub oak and brushlands beautifully blends into the lushness of the Laguna Mountains. Dominating the landscape are Jeffrey pines and live oaks, often providing peaceful shade beside lakes, rivers, and smaller streams.

Undoubtedly one of the most challenging sections of the PCT is in Anza-Borrego Desert State Park, California's largest. Named for Spanish explorer Juan Bautista de Anza and the area's bighorn sheep (*borrego* means "sheep" in Spanish), the desert is populated with 600 species of plants and 350 species of wildlife.

For experienced hikers, the waterless climb from Scissors Crossing to Warner Springs skirts San Felipe Hills and is infamous for its blistering temperatures and lack of shade. Despite the sun-baked soil, this region boasts distinctive plant life, including flowering prickly pear cactus, teddy-bear cholla, and fire-red ocotillo, some as tall as 15 feet. The desert terrain continues to CA 74, before gradually ascending to staggering elevations of more than 9,000 feet at San Jacinto Peak.

Featured in the second half of this book, The San Jacinto Mountains are two hours east of Los Angeles and two hours north of San Diego. This magnificent range spans 30 miles from the San Bernardino Mountains to the Santa Rosa Mountains. Here, the PCT fluctuates in elevation from 1,195 to 9,030 feet. This area is known for its pine forests, crystalline boulders, green meadows, rugged peaks, granite ridges, and abundant streams. Because of the elevation, snow often remains on parts of the trail through May.

Continuing north into the San Gorgonio Wilderness and the San Bernadino Mountains, you will share the trail with abundant wildlife. The San Bernardino Mountains have more than 75 species of mammals, 2,000 species of plants, 267 species of birds, and 55 species of reptiles. Among the most intriguing types of wildlife seen here are the coyote, mountain lion, and rattlesnake (prominent from April through June).

Beyond the breathtaking views of Big Bear Lake lies the foreboding wilderness of the San Gabriel Mountains and the contrasting terrain of the Angeles National Forest, which ranges from dense chaparral to pine-and-fir-covered slopes. Amazingly, this raw patch of nature is just 45 minutes from the bustle of downtown Los Angeles.

| Marking the way to Warner Springs

How to Use This Book

Use the **overview map** at the beginning of this book to assess the exact location of each hike's primary trailhead. Each hike's number appears on the overview map, on the map key beside the overview map, and in the Table of Contents. A hike's full profile is easy to locate as you flip through the book: Just match it with the hike number at the top of each page.

The hikes in this book include trails in four counties (San Diego, Riverside, San Bernardino, and Los Angeles) and in eleven regions: Campo Indian Reservation Area, Hauser Wilderness, Laguna Mountains, Cuyamaca Rancho State Park, Anza-Borrego Desert, San Felipe Wilderness, San Jacinto Wilderness, San Gorgonio Wilderness, San Bernardino Forest, San Gabriel Mountains, and Angeles National Forest.

Throughout the book, three types of **trails** are shown: loops, links to and from the PCT, and in-and-out segments of the PCT. Trail distances indicate complete lengths for loops and round-trips for everything else. Descriptions and map icons for trails of 12 miles or more cite campgrounds or campsites. For many trails of fewer than 12 miles, the text also provides camping information if there are noteworthy sites along the way. This is particularly useful for hikers who wish to link several short trail segments for continuous hiking of more than a day.

Each hike contains a detailed **map** that shows the trailhead, the route, significant features, facilities, and topographic landmarks such as creeks, overlooks, and peaks. While hiking, I used a GPS unit (Garmin eTrex) to gather map data and downloaded it into a digital mapping program (Topo USA). Without GPS, readers can easily access all trailheads in this book by using the directions given, the overview map, and the trail map, which typically shows at least one major road leading into the area.

With each hike's description, an **elevation profile** corresponds to the trail map. The profile provides a quick look at the trail from the side, enabling you to assess climbing ease or difficulty by visualizing how the terrain rises and falls.

Each trailhead's **GPS coordinates** are included with each profile. The data, collected during hikes with my handheld GPS unit, was downloaded and plotted onto a digital USGS topo map. Fortunately the PCT is well marked, meaning you most likely won't be needing GPS coordinates to navigate the trail. However, for readers who own a GPS unit, the latitude and longitude coordinates provided for each hike may be entered into the GPS unit, allowing you to navigate directly to the trailhead.

Without GPS, readers can easily access all trailheads in this book by using the directions given, the overview map, and the trail map. It is also recommended that for thru-hikes or longer trips on the PCT, hikers purchase a commercial topographic map. Regional maps can usually be purchased at ranger stations and outdoor equipment stores. To download maps with waypoints and data, visit www.pctmap.net.

The **Hike Profile** section for each hike includes maps and driving directions to a parking area convenient to the trailhead from a major road. Each section also provides "At a Glance" information for eight categories: hiking distance, approximate hiking time, trail highlights, scenery, trail condition, family friendly (appropriateness for children), difficulty of hike, and quality of solitude. Five of the categories are rated using a five-arrow (▲) system. Below is an example:

As noted above, mileages listed in the profiles refer to round-trip distance for linear segments and one-way distance in the case of loop hikes. If shuttling back from the mid-way point is an option, directions and mileage are profiled accordingly. Hiking times are based on an average walking speed of 2 to 3 miles per hour, with time built in for brief rests and pauses at overlooks. Times for hikes of 12 miles or more (considered overnight hikes) account for the effort of carrying a backpack.

Distance: 2 miles round-trip

Hiking time: 1 hour

Trail highlights: Swimming holes, effortless descent, oak-shaded banks

Difficulty: ▲ ▲

Family friendly: ▲ ▲ ▲

Scenery: ▲ ▲

Solitude: ▲ ▲

Trail condition: ▲ ▲ ▲

Following the estimate of the hiking time is a brief summary of unique characteristics and highlights of that trail. The two arrows for "difficulty" assure you that it is a relatively straightforward hike (five arrows would signal that it's strenuous). Three arrows for "family friendly" alert you that children would likely enjoy the hike. The two arrows for "scenery" indicate that it is relatively picturesque. With two arrows for "solitude," you can expect to encounter several other hikers on the trail. (With one arrow for solitude, you may well be elbowing your way up the trail, whereas with five arrows, you would be alone.) Three arrows for "trail condition" denote that it is typically in good shape. (One arrow would mean the trail is likely to be muddy, rocky, overgrown, or otherwise compromised.)

Below the "At a Glance" section are specific directions on how to reach the trailhead. Following the "Overview" summary, a more detailed narrative follows, in which trail junctions, stream crossings, and trailside features are noted, along with their distances from the trailhead. Flip through the book, read the descriptions, and choose a hike that appeals to you.

Weather

With PCT elevations ranging from 1,200 to more than 9,000 feet, the fluctuations in ecosystems can have a dramatic impact on the weather, water supply, and temperature. From the Mexican border to Lake Morena, the terrain is rather arid. Ironically, the Laguna Mountains, just 20 miles away, are dotted with small lakes and rivers and are sprinkled with snow until late spring. This diversity of terrain and landscape is typical of the Southern California portion of the PCT, with its broad range of ecosystems. Beyond the Lagunas, the trail enters the dry Anza-Borrego Desert before climbing the lush San Jacinto mountains. Elevations plunge yet again at San Gorgonio Wilderness, making this section passable even during winter months. In the heart of the San Bernardino Forest, the PCT gives way to rewarding views near Big Bear Lake. The final stretch crosses the San Gabriel Mountains near Cajon Pass and then traverses the chaparral valleys of the Angeles National Forest.

Generally, one can assume that 1,000 feet in elevation will result in a temperature change of 3 to 5 degrees. The PCT enters a transition zone before approaching Mount Laguna, which results in a dramatic alteration in scenery. Leaving behind brushy hillsides, the trail enters a cool, mountainous area of oaks and pines. Although not as high as the peaks of the San Bernardinos, the peaceful Laguna Mountains draw ocean moisture eastward to create precipitation.

| View of Morena Reservoir

At 6,000 feet, this area is often blanketed in snow through May. In fact, the Lagunas receive the most snowfall of any area in San Diego County. Winter nights can bring unexpected storms and freezing temperatures, which can lead to hypothermia for those who are unprepared. During the spring, the Laguna Mountains experience high winds with gusts up to 30 mph. Frontal storms are more prevalent in the northern regions. These storms tend to hit Southern California in late November. By December, snow will have covered higher elevations, and it will not begin to melt until May.

April thunderstorms are more common in the San Jacintos and the San Bernardinos, usually striking between 2 and 7 P.M. If rain clouds begin to roll in, look for shelter and a safe place to wait until lightning passes.

The ideal time for anyone to hike these higher elevations is June—after the snow melts and before the heat of summer is at its hottest. Thru-hikers headed for the PCT's northern terminus at the Canadian border should plan to launch from the Mexican border no later than mid-April. By this time, streams will be gushing and winter's remnants will slowly be fading into the warmth of May. No matter what time of year you hit the trail, check the weather forecast and plan accordingly—conditions are often unpredictable in mountain areas.

Safety

From blisters and dehydration to sunburns and bites, consequences can result from the risks we take as hikers. The best policy is to educate ourselves about how to prevent and/or avoid problems, prepare for adventure, and plan accordingly.

✛ FIRST AID

For any hiker, first-aid training or a refresher class in this field is well worth the time and cost. In addition to cardiopulmonary resuscitation (CPR) training, consider American Red Cross courses that teach the basics of treating wounds and broken bones and handling other trail emergencies. Be sure to pack a first-aid kit, especially for overnight hikes. Below is a list of recommended supplies:

- Antidiarrheal tablets
- Antihistamine tablets
- Antimicrobial ointment
- Antiseptic cleansing pads
- Athletic tape
- Elastic bandage
- Gauze pads
- Hydrocortisone
- Irrigation syringe
- Painkiller tablets
- Pocketknife, scissors, tweezers
- Povidine iodine
- Safety pins
- Snake bite kit
- Sunscreen, lip balm
- Water-resistant adhesive strips

The contents of your first-aid kit will vary depending on personal needs, terrain, weather, and duration of your hike. Pack a list of emergency phone numbers, and know where the nearest medical center is located. Although most hikers carry cell phones, service is usually limited in backcountry areas, so don't expect to have a connection.

✛ BLISTERS

Among the most common injuries are foot blisters, which can easily be avoided. Although small, these painful irritations can ruin a perfect hike. Make sure your shoes or boots are well broken in prior to hitting the trail. Try wearing thin, moisture-wicking socks that dry quickly, unlike cotton socks. During breaks, shake debris from shoes and socks; it can often lead to chafing.

Blisters that are filled with fluid should be drained only if the hike is far from over. To safely puncture a blister, apply antiseptic to the wound and prick the blister with a sterilized needle held at an angle. Avoid sticky bandages, as they may painfully peel away loose skin. To limit foot injuries, keep your feet dry, clean, and well rested whenever possible.

✛ WATER

The single most important item when hiking is water. In the Southern California portion of the PCT, some water sources are as much as 20 miles apart. The hunt for water can be daunting, especially in sections of Anza-Borrego Desert, where temperatures can exceed 100°F. A hydration backpack that holds up to 3 liters (100 ounces) of water is the best way to stay hydrated. Plan to drink about a liter of water for every five miles hiked. For longer distances, bring extra water bottles and pack purifying iodine tablets for water extracted from rivers and streams. Although water sources are listed throughout this book, updated information on water caches and water reports can be found at www.4jeffrey.net/pctwater.

While mountain water might appear crystal-clear, it may actually be contaminated by fertilizers, pesticides, or parasites. Prior to drinking any water, purify it with a filter, treat it with iodine, or boil it for at least five minutes. Another option is a lightweight purification wand that can clean a quart of water in two minutes with beams of ultraviolet light.

⊕ WILDFIRES

In Southern California, wildfires are virtually inevitable, especially during autumn, when Santa Ana winds blow. In October 2007, more than 1,500 homes were lost and more than 500,000 acres were burned by wildfires. The blazes were attributed to fallen power lines and arson. The PCT suffered damage again in May 2012, when the Banner Fire destroyed 2,851 acres. In September of that same year, the Campo fires burned 5,321 acres and 20 homes near the Mexican border.

In general, campfires are not allowed anywhere along the PCT's Southern California section. Only in designated car-camping areas are they permitted, and even then, fires must be contained within a fire ring. Water should always be on hand to extinguish the fire if necessary, and hot coals should be doused at least 30 minutes prior to campsite departure. Stir the water into the ashes, and check that they are not hot before you leave camp.

| Entering a cattle gate on the PCT

| Camping in the San Jacinto Mountains. Photo by Justin McChesney.

✚ BORDER TRAFFIC

In areas near the Mexican border, it is not uncommon to cross paths with undocumented migrants and Border Patrol agents. Hauser Canyon's valleys and creeks are a popular hideout for those hiking in and out of Mexico. It is always wise to hike with a partner and stick to the trail.

✚ WILDLIFE

Fortunately, hikers along the Southern California section of the PCT rarely encounter dangerous wildlife. The greatest risks are bee stings and rattlesnake bites. For those who are prone to allergic reactions, hike with an EpiPen, and have a snake bite kit on hand. Generally rattlesnakes warn victims before striking, unless they are caught off guard. If you are bitten, immediately head to your nearest medical facility, or use a snake bite kit to remove venom until you can be properly treated. Although mountain lions do live in wilderness areas, they are generally afraid of humans and stay far from the trails. In California, there have been a total of 15 mountain lion attacks on humans since 1890, of which six have been fatal. If you encounter a mountain lion, stand tall, shout aggressively, and throw stones to scare away the animal. Hiking with a partner is the best way to deter such occurrences.

✪ GENERAL SAFETY

- Inform a friend or family member where you will be hiking and the duration of your trip.
- Do not rely on cell phones in back-country areas since signals are weak and inconsistent.
- Always carry food and water, no matter how long the hike.
- Bring potable water, or treat water before drinking it from its source.
- Stay on designated trails.
- Be aware of your surroundings.
- Hike with emergency supplies (headlamp, lighter, whistle, warm clothing, and waterproof covering).
- Protect yourself from the sun.
- Wear bright colors during hunting season.
- If hiking with children, keep them close.
- Know how to recognize and treat poison oak, rattlesnake bites, and ticks.

Hiking Tips

The combination of fresh air, stunning landscape, and invigorating exercise serves as a catalyst for enjoying the Southern California portion of the PCT. There are, however, several tips that can help make your hike an even more unforgettable experience. Adhere to all hiking etiquette rules, and follow the outdoor ethic of "take only pictures, leave only footprints."

➤ PLAN AHEAD

Because of past wildfires, Southern California's trails have taken a beating, but they have finally started to show signs of recovery. During seasonal blazes, sections of the PCT are often closed, forcing hikers to detour via designated routes. Those who trespass into fire areas are not only breaking the law but are also putting their lives at risk, as winds can shift flames at any moment. Even distant fires have a tendency to rapidly spread, making it difficult to breathe, due to thick smoke. In addition to flames, other dangers include falling trees, the spraying of retardant chemicals, and hot spots that remain underground after flames have been extinguished.

For current fire information, visit www.inciweb.org. Being informed of trail conditions is critical to planning, especially when unexpected storms are passing through. Pack accordingly, notify others of your whereabouts, and always bring a first-aid kit. Updated weather reports and water source information can be found at the Pacific Crest Trail Association website, www.pcta.org.

➤ ALLOW PLENTY OF TIME

Regardless of one's level of fitness, the PCT has a tendency to humble virtually any hiker, especially when crossing the desert. When planning a trip, take into account elevation, weather, and potential detours that may slow the pace. You may even want to allot time for an afternoon break or the exploration of spur trails. If possible, start the hike early enough so that you can take your time and still have plenty of daylight at the end of the hike.

● AVOID BUSY WEEKENDS

Hiking on weekdays is much more enjoyable than on Saturdays and Sundays, when trails are often packed with weekend warriors. To limit your rush-hour experience, begin early in the morning and consider hiking on overcast days. Sometimes a looming cloud has the power to clear the trails. Be sure to check weather conditions before hitting the road, and pack a jacket for unexpected changes in temperatures, especially in mountain areas.

● POWER UP

Never curtail your food and water intake when hiking long distances. Depending on one's pace and elevation, hiking burns 350 to 500 calories per hour. Quick power snacks are essential and can sustain energy during grueling climbs. Whether you take trail mix and apples or energy bars and beef jerky, a few extra goodies can keep you powered up. Above all, drink plenty of water.

● PACK ACCORDINGLY

Prepare for sudden changes in weather, and be sure to pack accordingly. Winter hikers will most likely need gaiters or heavy boots to stay dry at higher elevations. During spring and summer, fabric hiking boots should suffice. Overnight hikers will want to pack a down sleeping bag that is both light and warm. For insulation and additional cushion, thin sleeping pads are also recommended.

● USE THE BUDDY SYSTEM

There is nothing quite like sharing the joys of the great outdoors with a friend. From enriching conversations and safety to photo ops and moral support, the benefits of hiking with a partner are endless. If you plan on setting out solo, stay on the trail, carry a cell phone, inform others of your location, and know all exit points in case of emergency.

Know about Permits and Restrictions

National Forest areas in Southern California require that hikers purchase a National Forest Adventure Pass. Valid for one year, an Adventure Pass costs $30, however it can also be purchased as a single day pass for $5. These must be displayed inside your vehicle windshield when parking at trailheads. Revenue is invested locally for on-the-ground projects. An Adventure Pass can be purchased at ranger stations and at local businesses near hiking areas. If you have the Interagency Annual Pass ($80 for entrance to national parks) you do not need to buy an Adventure Pass since it covers these fees. To learn more about permits, visit www.fs.fed.us.

Because the PCT is a nonmechanized trail, the Forest Service prohibits bicycles and motorized vehicles. The trail can be accessed only by foot or by horse. Leashed dogs are allowed on all trails throughout this book, except in the San Jacinto State Park Wilderness. In addition to displaying the Adventure Pass, you will need a USFS permit to enter the San Jacinto area, available free of charge through www.fsva.org.

The San Jacinto State Park issues wilderness camping permits up to two months in ad-

| Morris Creek sparkles in the distance

vance for Round Valley, Tamarack Valley, and Strawberry Junction. However, campfires and dogs are not permitted in the State Wilderness. To obtain a permit, contact the head office in Idyllwild at 951-659-2607 or visit www.parks.ca.gov.

Since the San Jacinto area is managed by the U.S. Forest Service and by California State Parks, you'll have to obtain a separate permit for camping in Skunk Cabbage, Tahquitz, Chinquapin, North Rim, Lower Basin, and Desert View. Permits are available up to 90 days in advance from the Idyllwild Ranger Station at 951-659-2117 or 909-382-2921. Permit applications are available at www.fsva.org.

If you plan to use a stove, lantern, or campfire outside a developed recreation area (which we do not recommend), be sure to obtain a free California Campfire Permit, valid for one year. They can be obtained at any Bureau of Land Management office or Forest Service office, ranger stations, visitors centers, or online at www.fs.usda.gov.

For the most part, trails featured in this book are clearly marked with PCT posts. Areas that require careful navigation are described in detail in each chapter. To report poor trail conditions, contact the PCTA at 888-PC-TRAIL.

For those hiking more than 500 consecutive miles, the Pacific Crest Trail Association will issue Long Distance Permits (www.pcta.org/discover-the-trail/permits/), free of charge. They are valid for overnight use on the PCT. To become a member of the Pacific Crest Trail Association (PCTA), download an application at www.pcta.org. Membership fees start at $35.

| Rocky view from Morena Butte |

PART I

Campo Indian Reservation Area, Hauser Wilderness, and Laguna Mountains

| Canadian thistle |

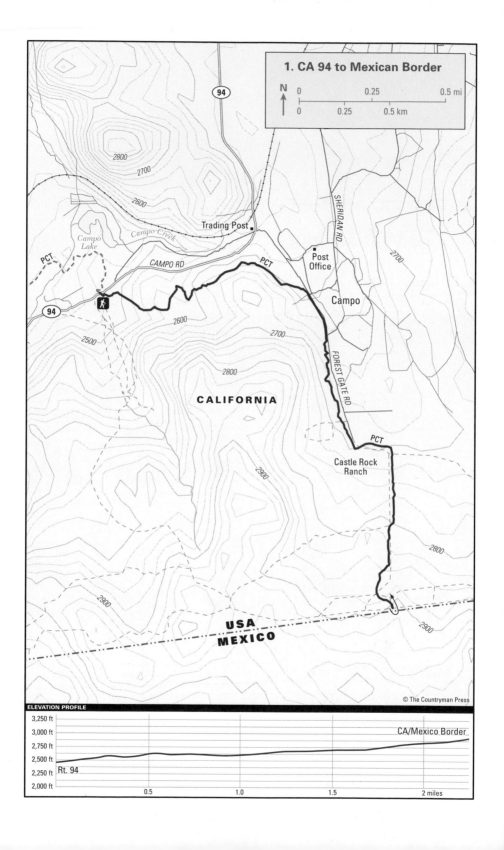

Hike 1

CA 94 to Mexican Border

Distance: 4.6 miles round-trip

Hiking time: 2–3 hours

Trail highlights: Proximity to Mexico, the Pacific Crest Trail Monument, a sense of utter accomplishment (or excitement) because this spot marks the beginning (or end) of the PCT

Difficulty: ▲

Family friendly: ▲

Scenery: ▲

Solitude: ▲▲

Trail condition: ▲▲

Getting There

Southbound hikers can access the PCT by exiting Interstate 8 onto CA 94. The unmarked trailhead begins just west of Campo on CA 94. At the time of this writing, the PCT post on the south side of the highway had been removed. To find the route, follow the jeep road that climbs east past several mailboxes.

To start from the Mexican border, head south off CA 94 on Forest Gate Road at Campo. After the Border Patrol Station, continue south past the Juvenile Ranch Facility, and turn south onto the dirt road that passes under power lines. Continue uphill to another dirt road that parallels the steel wall that divides the United States from Mexico. There is parking northwest of the PCT monument. Be sure to notify Border Patrol officers of your planned route and intended parking place.

GPS TRAILHEAD COORDINATES

UTM Zone	11S
Easting	548484
Northing	3607671
Latitude	N32.60549°
Longitude	W116.48327°

| California buckwheat near the Mexican border

Overview

Safety, supplies, and seasons are three key elements to consider when hiking near the Mexican border. It is best to embark in late April or early May, when cold nights have faded and blistering heat has yet to arrive. For those who intend to continue north toward Hauser Canyon, be sure to stock up on water in Campo. The next supply station is Morena Village, a grueling 20 miles away.

Overall, this 2.3-mile stretch between Mexico and Campo is not a picturesque afternoon stroll. Unlike most of Southern California's often-beautiful 650 miles of the PCT, this brief section follows a dusty road lined with omnipresent chaparral. At times, the trail is poorly marked, dropping into washed-out sand pits that parallel a dirt road leading to the border. Beyond CA 94, the route traverses dry hillsides and passes through the small town of Campo. For those heading south, it is the final leg of the hike, ascending toward the six-foot steel border wall that makes the adventure intriguingly surreal. Spring hiking might result in some trail traffic, as many PCT thru-hikers tend to launch their journey to Canada in April, with approximately half of them making it to the end.

Although far from spectacular in landscape, this route is a must for anyone who has hiked a significant amount of the PCT and longs to see the official launching point of the road less traveled.

In Detail

Begin on CA 94, just west of Campo. On this desolate road, a group of mailboxes marks the southbound launching point. This section of the PCT is poorly marked and devoid of signage at the time of writing. Head east along the washed-out jeep trail, and fork right (southeast) at the first divide.

| Touching Mexico

You'll slightly ascend over the brushy slopes of chamise, sagebrush, and yucca. At the 0.28-mile mark, the trail begins to drop, offering views of Campo in the distance. Now approaching the town, the route crosses a gray granite slab before dropping onto paved Forest Gate Road. Walk on the west shoulder past several homes and the Border Patrol Station. The PCT branches off

at 1.66 miles. Bend to the right and head south on the thick, sandy trail that parallels the dirt road. This area may take a bit of patience, as the way is not clearly defined.

Just before 2.0 miles, the trail passes under power lines to cross the dirt road. You will now be able to clearly see the border wall. Along the way, expect to be left in a cloud of dust created by a passing truck from the Border Patrol, or be eyed by the Minutemen, a group of volunteers with the announced goal of supporting enforcement of immigration laws.

After a final section of yarrow and shrubs, the path joins the dirt road that parallels the Mexican border. Once you reach the wall, walk east toward the PCT Monument, constructed of five 12-by-12-inch posts. Engraved on the posts is the elevation: 2,915 feet; the distance to Canada: 2,627 miles; and the date of the trail's establishment by an act of Congress: October 2, 1968. Built into the monument is a cradle, which holds a journal where hikers can sign their names. This is an excellent photo opportunity as you begin or conclude your journey on the Pacific Crest Trail.

For northbound hikers, this trail begins at the PCT monument and can connect to Hike #2 at Hauser Canyon.

near Rancho del Campo, once a World War I cavalry camp. Today, the grounds serve as a ranch facility for juvenile offenders.

Throughout the year, this overgrown section is lined with blue-eyed grass and white popcorn-like blossoms. At 1.5 miles, the trail T's with a dirt road at Castle Rock Ranch. Cross the road to enter a wide, grassy field. A second dirt road intersects

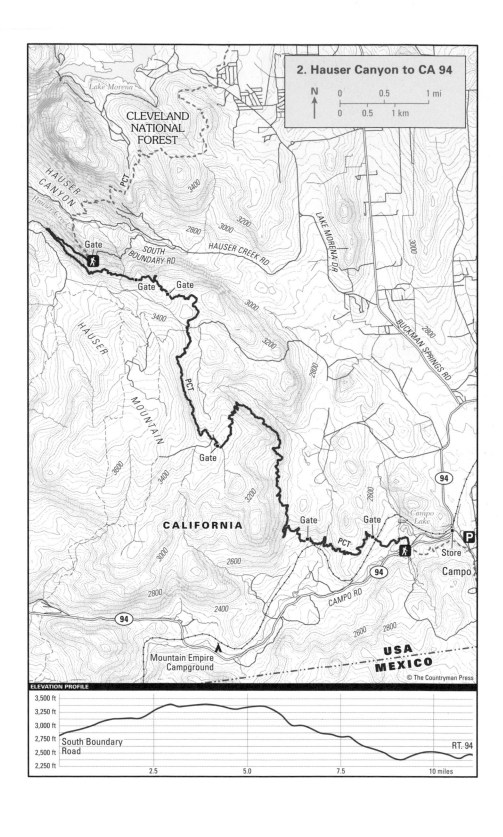

N

| 0 | | 0.5 | | 1 mi |

| 0 | 0.5 | | 1 km |

Lake Morena

CLEVELAND
NATIONAL
FOREST

PCT

HAUSER
CANYON

Hauser Creek

3400

2800   3000   3200

HAUSER CREEK RD

LAKE MORENA DR

3000

Gate

SOUTH
BOUNDARY RD

Gate   Gate

2800

BUCKMAN SPRINGS RD

3400

3000

3200

H
A
U
S
E
R

M
O
U
N
T
A
I
N

PCT

2800

3600   3400

Gate

3200

94

CALIFORNIA

3000

Gate   Gate

2600

Campo
Lake

PCT

P

Store

Campo

2600

2800

94

94

2400

CAMPO RD

2600   2800

94

Mountain Empire
Campground

USA

MEXICO

© The Countryman Press

ELEVATION PROFILE

| 3,500 ft |
| 3,250 ft |
| 3,000 ft |
| 2,750 ft | South Boundary |
| 2,500 ft | Road |
| 2,250 ft |

RT. 94

2.5   5.0   7.5   10 miles

Hike 2

Hauser Canyon to CA 94

Distance: 23.8 miles round-trip

Hiking time: 11 hours

Trail highlights: Canyon views, shaded cottonwood field, creekside knoll

Difficulty: ▲▲▲▲

Family friendly: ▲

Scenery: ▲▲

Solitude: ▲▲▲▲

Trail condition: ▲▲▲

Getting There

If you're planning a one-way route south, reaching the start of this hike will take some transportation assistance (hitching a ride) since there is no designated parking in Hauser Canyon. Take the Buckman Springs Road exit from Interstate 8. Turn right onto Highway 94, and continue 1.5 miles to Forrest Gate Road. Turn left, and park at the Campo Post Office, located on the corner of Forrest Gate and Jeb Stewart Road.

With approval, you can also park across the street at the Campo Fire Station. After you park, hitch a ride to South Boundary Road, off of Hauser Creek Road, south of Lake Morena. The hike described below begins on the east side of this jeep road, 2 miles past a metal gate, where the PCT climbs out of Hauser Canyon (W 32° 39' 605"). From here, the PCT will briefly merge with the jeep road before branching south. Northbound hikers can access the PCT

by taking I-8 to CA 94. The trailhead begins just west of Campo, a small town 2 miles from the Mexican border. For the brave round-trip hiker, park near Buckman Springs Road (for southbound) or in Campo (for northbound), and return in the direction from which you came.

GPS TRAILHEAD COORDINATES

UTM Zone	11S
Easting	542902
Northing	3613102
Latitude	N32.65472°
Longitude	W116.54252°

Overview

This hike picks up where the Lake Morena–Hauser Canyon hike leaves off. (See Hike 3: Lake Morena to Hauser Canyon.) From this section's starting point, the PCT runs north 6 miles to Lake Morena County Park. A "there-and-back" from CA 94 to South Boundary Road at Hauser Wilderness Area makes for a challenging 23.8-mile hike.

From this ridge-top launching point, the trail goes south toward Hauser Mountain, through chaparral slopes draped in bright orange dodder, commonly known as "witch's hair" due to its stringy appearance.

The trail is more manageable southbound because of the gradual descent and the cottonwood groves that break up the sporadic inclines. The beauty of the hike lies in its trailside subtleties: an old wooden bridge, spring wildflowers, peeling manzanitas, rock formations, and lush ravines.

Because of the proximity of Mexico, be prepared to encounter Border Patrol officers and illegal immigrants. PCT hikers might want to register with the Immigration and Naturalization Service office in Campo to avoid confusion.

When camping, avoid Hauser Creek to the north, where undocumented immigrants generally hide during the day because of its shade and water. For those who are connecting Hikes 1, 2, and 3, try to complete the entire segment from Lake Morena to Campo in a single day. Plan to camp in either of these small-town areas rather than in the desolate, often waterless area in between (the creek is usually dry by April).

Be sure to stock up on water in Campo

or Lake Morena County Park. Other than the sometimes-dry Hauser Creek, the first available water when hiking north is 18 miles from Campo. Regardless of the direction, the hike brutally dishes up dry terrain, shadeless switchbacks, steep elevations, and grueling climbs. The difficulty of the journey makes the completion a rewarding one.

In Detail

From South Boundary Road, begin at the vintage PCT post engraved with the distance north to Lake Morena (although this hike is southbound). The trail links with this dirt road for 0.63 miles before breaking south and narrowing. At the time of this writing, the PCT emblem was missing from the wooden post where GPS coordinates show the southbound split at W 116° 33' 43."

From here, the trail slightly ascends, of-

| San Diego and Arizona Eastern Railway tracks

fering impressive views of Hauser Canyon to the northwest. Spring wildflowers are prevalent in the first mile, giving way to poodle-dog bush, scarlet bugler, Canadian thistle, larkspur, and sticky leaf monkey flower. Here, the blazing sun takes its toll on manzanitas, which shed their mahogany-colored bark in curled sheets.

A wall of towering boulders leads to several switchbacks heading southeast. After dropping into a shallow wash, the trail slightly ascends toward a spectacular canyon view. In the distance, you can see the PCT snaking down from Lake Morena. For those hiking from that area, the vision of where the trip began is extremely rewarding.

Just before 2 miles, the trail crosses a pipe gate, leaving behind any sign of Hauser Canyon. The path soon cuts through blankets of chaparral, perfumed with the familiar scent of white sage. Shortly thereafter, you will pass through a second metal gate. Remember to close the gates behind you so that cattle do not escape.

At 3.5 miles, cross a jeep road and continue slightly southwest, where olive-colored hills are vibrantly splashed with orange dodder. This hairy, parasitic plant (known as "witch's hair") drapes shrubs throughout Southern California.

The trail finally provides a brief section of shade, mostly from chamise, just after the 5-mile mark. Beyond that, you'll cross a dirt road and continue south. What started as clusters of witch's hair now envelop entire slopes with blankets of orange string from May through July.

After a third gate, the trail dips into a wash and starts to descend at 6 miles. This much-appreciated drop in elevation comes with several switchbacks that skirt Hauser Mountain. The next mile continues to descend past gigantic boulder slabs that seem to melt onto the trail. To the southeast, you can begin to see Campo near CA 94.

Now approaching 8 miles, hikers are taunted with vistas of a distant pond and shaded Star Ranch. In September 2010, these hillsides were engulfed in flames after lost immigrants started a signal fire and burned over 800 acres.

You'll traverse several rock slabs that cover the trail before cutting inland toward a pleasant field of wild grass. Yet another pipe gate crosses the route. Brittlebrush and white yarrow lead the way to a ravine of cottonwoods, willows, and poison oak. The creek here tends to flow only during winter. Pass through another metal gate, and then cross the San Diego and Arizona Eastern Railway tracks.

As you complete 11 miles, follow the trail to the left as it enters a grove of cottonwoods. This is by far the greenest section of the entire hike. Crossing the seldom-flowing Campo Creek is a pleasant wooden bridge built from telephone poles in 1994.

Continue on the PCT until the trail bends left toward the two-lane highway CA 94. Having completed 11.9 miles, either retrace your steps to South Boundary Road or treat yourself to a cold drink at the historic Campo Stone Store. Located 0.3 miles north at the Forest Gate Road junction, this convenience store dates back to 1885 and is worth a visit if you have the time.

Just 3 miles west of the store is the Mountain Empire Campground. Conveniently located 0.75 miles west of the PCT, the campgrounds offer restrooms, showers, laundry facilities, and 14 campsites (no reservations required). Avoid visiting Campo between October and February, when nights are cold. The campgrounds are located at 29146 Highway 94 in Campo. For more information, call 619-478-5207.

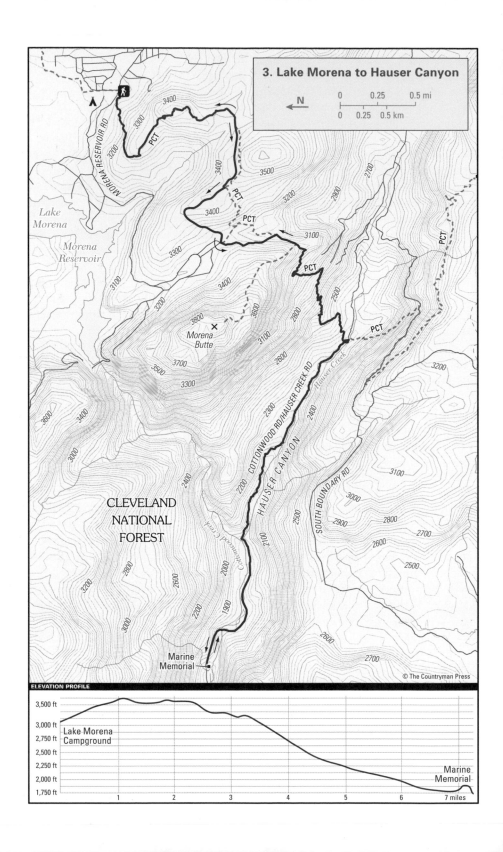

3. Lake Morena to Hauser Canyon

N

| 0 | 0.25 | 0.5 mi |
| 0 | 0.25 | 0.5 km |

3400
3300
3200
PCT
MORENA RESERVOIR RD

Lake
Morena

Morena
Reservoir

3100
3200
3300
3400
3500
3700
3300
3600
3400
3000
2400
2600
2800
3200
3000

× Morena
Butte
3800

3600
3100
2600
2800
3500
3400
3100
3200
2900
2700

3500
3200
PCT
PCT
PCT
3100
2500
PCT
2800
2600
2300
PCT
2700
PCT
3200

Hauser Creek
COTTONWOOD RD/HAUSER CREEK RD
HAUSER CANYON
2400
2500
SOUTH BOUNDARY RD
3100
3000
2900
2800
2700
2600
2500

CLEVELAND
NATIONAL
FOREST

Cottonwood Creek
2200
2100
2000
1900
1900

2600
2700

Marine
Memorial

© The Countryman Press

ELEVATION PROFILE

3,500 ft
3,000 ft
2,750 ft   Lake Morena
2,500 ft   Campground
2,250 ft
2,000 ft
1,750 ft

Marine
Memorial

1   2   3   4   5   6   7 miles

Hike 3

Lake Morena to Hauser Canyon

Distance: 14 miles round-trip	
Hiking time: 8 hours	
Trail highlights: Creekside sycamores, oak-filled meadows, freshwater pools	
Difficulty: ▲▲▲▲	
Family friendly: ▲	
Scenery: ▲▲▲	
Solitude: ▲▲▲▲	
Trail condition: ▲▲▲	

GPS TRAILHEAD COORDINATES	
UTM Zone	11S
Easting	545268
Northing	3616200
Latitude	N32.68257°
Longitude	W116.51713°

Getting There

Exit Interstate 8 at Buckman Springs Road, and head west toward Lake Morena County Park. Turn right on Oak Drive and right again at Lake Morena Drive. Head 0.8 mile to the county campground, where a shaded dirt area to the left offers space for approximately five cars. Additional parking is available along the paved road. A PCT post marks the trailhead, off the parking area.

For parking inside Lake Morena County Park, a small day-use fee is required; parking outside this area requires an Adventure Pass, available by the day for $5. For those who plan to overnight in this region, Lake Morena County Park has a designated campground ($20/night) and decent bass and trout fishing at Lake Morena (fishing permits $5/day). Lake Morena County Park is located at 2550 Lake Morena Drive. For more information, call 619-478-5473.

| Lupine at Hauser Canyon

Overview

The difference between hiking Hauser Canyon in spring versus any other time of year is as dramatic as the difference between a watercolor painting and a black and white print. In late March, the chaparral slopes are splattered with vibrant wildflowers in bright shades of yellow, purple, blue, and white.

After passing Lake Morena, the trail switches back several times before dipping into an oak-filled valley. As if embarking on an entirely new journey, the hiker then descends into the canyon, past rose-colored boulders and rocky ridges. One of the many highlights is the distant view of Barrett Lake cradled to the west.

At the canyon floor is an old dirt road traversed only by hikers, undocumented immigrants and the Border Patrol. Even during peak season, this hike offers solitude because of its outbound ascent and its length. Those who commit to it are rewarded with a midway, creekside walk past freshwater pools and shaded meadows.

In Detail

From the PCT trailhead, follow the trail west, past Lake Morena. This 2-square-mile lake sets the backdrop for the wildflowers that dot the trail in spring. Yellow goldfields, common tansy, baby blue eyes, and purple peony add color to the stark white clusters of lemonade berry and wild cucumber blossoms.

Before completing the first mile, the trail has several switchbacks with gradual ascents in between. Butterflies, hawks, lizards, horned toads, and beetles make themselves known on this long trek. Granite slabs sprouting agave, yucca, and prickly pear cactus envelop entire slopes.

At 1.6 miles, a spur trail merges from the east. When returning to the trailhead at the end of the hike, remember to stay left at this fork. Less than one hundred feet past this point, head right at the next trail split. The left trail is shorter, but it misses the picturesque valley filled with live oaks.

On reaching the shaded valley, turn left at the small wooden post marked "PCT 1.5." This overgrown path parallels Morena Butte (see Hike 4). Rather drab in winter, this section of the trail comes alive in spring with purple owl's clover, mission bells, yellow buttercups, and Indian paintbrush. Gradually, the trail traverses the southeast side of Morena Butte. Offering views in both directions, the path divides the valley to the left and pink-hued boulders to the right.

| Admiring Lake Morena

In a startling change of scenery, the hike dips into Hauser Canyon and snakes slightly west along a rugged trail. The magnificence of nature can be seen in the sapphire waters of Barrett Lake in the distance. Like tiny pebbles strewn on a hill, massive boulders dot the mountains, making one feel dwarfed in their presence. Throughout the 900-foot descent, several rock platforms serve as ideal spots to rest and luxuriate in the panoramic view. Remnants of undocumented-immigrant hideouts, such as Mexican blankets and canned food, can be found in numerous caves that burrow into the canyon walls.

Despite the arid terrain, the lavender lupines, harebells, and white forget-me-nots

add striking displays of color in season. At the base of the canyon, the narrow, rocky trail spills onto Hauser Creek Road. Leave the PCT and head west (right), with the creek always to the left.

Offering a refreshing change in landscape, the peaceful stroll along this stretch is shaded with towering oaks and speckled sycamores. The farther you travel, the more spectacular the flowers become, especially in late March. Wild pea, morning glory, and Indian paintbrush give way to an entire slope blanketed in lavender wildflowers. During the spring, the brilliance is unparalleled, right down to the hillsides of chaparral splashed with deep blue ceanothus.

Just after 6 miles, Cottonwood Creek arrives from Morena Dam (2 miles north), creating several freshwater pools. It flows west through Hauser Canyon and eventually meets at Barrett Lake Reservoir, the same lake visible from the canyon ridge

Cross the usually trickling water to enter the former Hauser Creek Campground, now a tranquil meadow filled with beautiful oaks. Although overnight hikers are welcome to camp in this clearing, they are discouraged from doing so due to the heavy illegal immigration traffic in this area. Also, any water taken from the nearby creek must be purified. Note that campfires are not permitted.

Continue past a concrete dam and fishpond until you reach the Marine Memorial plaque at 7 miles. The plaque pays tribute to nine Marine firefighters who gave their lives during the California wildfires of 1943.

This memorial marks the turnaround point. For the return hike, be sure to have plenty of water, as the climb out of the valley is arid, steep, and devoid of shade. Retrace your steps out of the canyon, back to the northbound PCT. Continue to the trailhead where your adventure began.

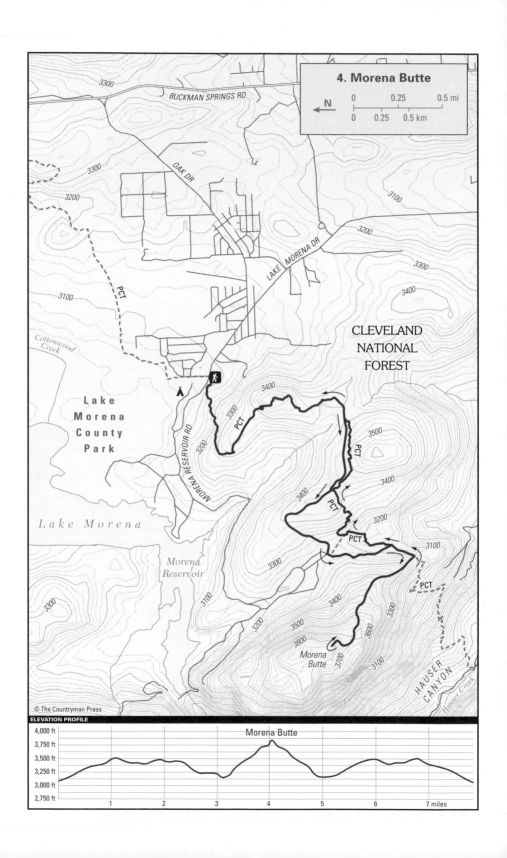

4. Morena Butte

| 0 | 0.25 | 0.5 mi |
| 0 | 0.25 | 0.5 km |

N

BUCKMAN SPRINGS RD

OAK DR

LAKE MORENA DR

PCT

3300
3300
3200
3100
3200
3100
3300
3400
3300
3400

Cottonwood
Creek

CLEVELAND
NATIONAL
FOREST

MADRENA RESERVOIR RD

PCT

3400
3300

3500

PCT

3400

Lake
Morena
County
Park

Lake Morena

PCT

3200

PCT

3100

PCT

Morena
Reservoir

3300
3100
3300

3400
3500
3800
3700

Morena
Butte

3600
3300
3100

3200

HAUSER CANYON

Hauser Creek

© The Countryman Press

ELEVATION PROFILE

Morena Butte

4,000 ft
3,750 ft
3,500 ft
3,250 ft
3,000 ft
2,750 ft

1   2   3   4   5   6   7 miles

Hike 4
Morena Butte

Distance: 8 miles round-trip	
Hiking time: 4 hours	
Trail highlights: Summit plateaus, lake	
views, granite slabs, oak-filled meadow	
Difficulty: ▲▲▲	
Family friendly: ▲▲	
Scenery: ▲▲▲	
Solitude: ▲▲▲	
Trail condition: ▲▲▲	

GPS TRAILHEAD COORDINATES

UTM Zone	11S
Easting	545268
Northing	3616200
Latitude	N32.68257°
Longitude	W116.51713°

Getting There

Exit Interstate 8 at Buckman Springs Road, and head west toward Lake Morena County Park. Turn right on Oak Drive and right again at Lake Morena Drive. Head 0.8 mile to the county campground, where a shaded dirt area to the left offers space for approximately five cars. Additional parking is available along the paved road or inside the park. A PCT post marks the trailhead, off the dirt parking area. A grassy knoll and a large oak provide an ideal spot to prepare for the journey.

For parking inside Lake Morena County Park, a small day-use fee is required; parking outside this area requires an Adventure Pass.

| A flowering **Our Lord's Candle** *(Hespero-yucca whipplei)*

Overview

The uniqueness of Morena Butte is in the dramatic divide of the two-part landscape. At first, hikers weave past Lake Morena, through rock fields and chaparral slopes. Then a pleasant meadow leads to a change in scenery, with scattered oaks. Offering one final taste of the just-traversed terrain, a shoulder looks out over an open rift before the trail climbs the southeast side of Morena Butte. A highlight of this journey is the ascent through manzanita "tunnels" that lead to boulders dominating the mountain. As one approaches all three summits, the well-marked trail disappears, making the rocky climb one of adventure and reward. Unlike many there-and-back trails, the Morena Butte hike offers the bonus of a scenic loop with a brush-filled center. This hike is best in spring and early summer, when wildflowers are on display.

In Detail

Begin by launching from the PCT post at the base of the parking area. Fifty yards into the ascent, veer right at the three-pronged fork and climb southwest, past gray boulders and thick chaparral. The first section of this journey is relatively level, with lovely views of the 2-square-mile lake below.

| Cloudy day at Morena Butte

Pass the side trail that splits off to the right and descends to the lake. Continue straight on the PCT trail as it gradually changes from packed dirt to a speckled, salt-and-pepper–like granite.

Along the way, the trail reveals stunning landscapes, such as a boulder platform that hangs high above Lake Morena. Running parallel to the water, the ascending trail sharply bends to the left before swinging south over the brushy slopes. Here, the trail widens slightly and takes on a more colorful look, with green shrubs and crimson rock paths. During the springtime, the hillside comes alive with lilac ceanothus, globemallow, and Our Lord's Candle—a type of yucca known as Hesperoyucca whipplei.

The area offers refuge to leaping crickets, singing birds, humming bees, and colonies of army ants. The occasional horned lizard can also be seen soaking in the afternoon sun. As lake views fade, massive rock platforms take aesthetic precedence, often

in less than a mile. Shaded oaks line the way to a perfect resting place. Birdwatchers might spot the occasional Phainopepla (silky black plumage with a pointed crest) or the Hooded Oriole (bright yellow-orange body with black wings). Continue as the trail bears left toward the dirt road marked by a "Morena Butte Trail" sign. Turn left onto the trail until it merges with the PCT again.

Just before the 3-mile point, an unmarked trail ascends the southeast shoulder of Morena Butte. The launching point for this difficult-to-find route is between the two PCT posts, just before the trail dips into Hauser Canyon. Cairn clusters point the way up the rocky one-mile-long path to the summits. In season, the arduous grade is dotted with yellow fiddleneck, campanula harebell, white forget-me-not, and hairy ceanothus.

Manzanita archways act as the conduit to granite slabs and massive boulders that dominate the trail. In the springtime, the soft pink blossoms of Our Lord's Candle contrast strikingly with their thorny eight-foot stalks.

Eventually the path fades and splits into three directions, identifiable only by small mounds of cairns. The climb over rocky ridges and tight passageways, offers spectacular views of Morena Reservoir below. If time permits, explore all three summits before ascending back to the PCT.

Once back on the main trail, retrace your steps until you reach the fork in the road. Rather than heading left and back toward the meadow, follow the PCT to the right. Forming the second half of the loop, the narrow path enters a mossy field. Spilling onto either side of the sandy trail are rock slabs sprouting with prickly pear cactus. The PCT eventually links back to the lake-view ridge where the hike began, offering beauty and shade in the final steps.

covering sections of the trail like hardened lava. Emerging around these plateaus are sagebrush, desert tobacco, and eucalyptus.

Be aware of the miniature stone walls that cross the path. They serve to divert water during the rainy season. Parts of the trail have eroded, forcing the hiker to walk inside a deep rut.

The trail splits from the PCT to join an old dirt road that dips into a peaceful valley. The brief detour will reconnect with the PCT

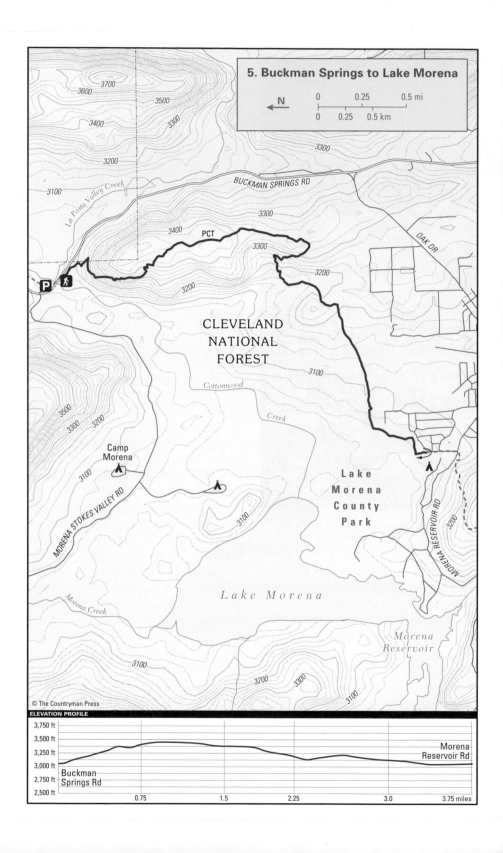

5. Buckman Springs to Lake Morena

N

| 0 | 0.25 | 0.5 mi |
| 0 | 0.25 | 0.5 km |

3700
3600
3500
3400
3300
3200
3100

La Posta Valley Creek

BUCKMAN SPRINGS RD

3300

3300

OAK DR

3400
PCT
3300

3200

3200

CLEVELAND
NATIONAL
FOREST

3100

Cottonwood

Creek

3500
3300
3200

Camp
Morena

3100

MORENA STOKES VALLEY RD

Lake
Morena
County
Park

MORENA RESERVOIR RD

3100

3200

Lake Morena

Morena Creek

*Morena
Reservoir*

3100

3200
3300
3100

© The Countryman Press

ELEVATION PROFILE

| 3,750 ft |
| 3,500 ft |
| 3,250 ft |
| 3,000 ft |
| 2,750 ft |
| 2,500 ft |

Morena
Reservoir Rd

Buckman
Springs Rd

0.75   1.5   2.25   3.0   3.75 miles

Hike 5

Buckman Springs to Lake Morena

Distance: 8 miles round-trip

Hiking time: 3.5 hours

Trail highlights: Lakeside campsite, granite boulders, shoreline trail

Difficulty: ▲

Family friendly: ▲▲

Scenery: ▲▲

Solitude: ▲

Trail condition: ▲▲▲

| Woolly Blue Curls *(Trichostema lanatum)*

Getting There

Exit Interstate 8 at Buckman Springs Road. Park at the 6.5-mile mark, between the Cottonwood Fire Station (3134 Buckman Springs Road) and the long, white bridge. On the left side of the road is a dirt turnout with space for approximately three cars. All cars must display a Wilderness Parking Pass. The trailhead begins directly below the white bridge at Cottonwood Creek.

For PCT hikers coming from the north, the Boulder Oaks Campground just east of Buckman Springs Road is a pleasant resting spot. Additional campsites and supplies can be found at Lake Morena County Park.

GPS TRAILHEAD COORDINATES	
UTM Zone	11S
Easting	546844
Northing	3619983
Latitude	N32.71662°
Longitude	W116.50014°

Overview

A child-friendly hike, this section of the Pacific Crest Trail conveniently begins and ends at campgrounds with picnic areas, freshwater, and shady oaks. Launching from Cottonwood Creek, the trail briefly parallels Buckman Springs Road before ascending a chaparral slope. From April through July, the arid landscape comes alive with scarlet buglers and Indian paintbrush. Distant views of Hauser Mountain and Lake Morena come and go around every bend. After crossing several jeep tracks, the trail skirts the shoreline and ends at beautiful Lake Morena.

In Detail

From Buckman Springs Road, find the trailhead just below the white bridge at the road's 6.5-mile mark. The PCT briefly parallels the bridge before crossing over Cottonwood Creek and under the bridge. Although generally not more than a trickle, the creek can reach high levels during the rainy season, which lasts from November through March. In that case, cross the bridge and begin the hike on the opposite side of the road.

Beyond the bridge, the trail narrows and enters an oak forest. This is the most colorful section of the trail, especially in spring, when grasslands are lined with popcorn-like yarrow, purple phacelia, and Indian paintbrush. Less than half a mile into the trek, the path bends west, steadily curving around mossy boulders. A series of switchbacks climb the ridge, leaving behind any sign of Buckman Springs Road. When in bloom, patches of purple lupine, daisy fleabane, blazing star, and Canadian thistle give way to large boulders that jut from chaparral slopes.

To the west, you can clearly see Lake Morena, the target of this journey. Follow the PCT posts along the slope, steadily climbing from Cottonwood Valley toward the Lake Morena area. About one mile into the trek, boulder platforms offer an ideal spot to admire the view.

Views of the lake briefly disappear behind hillsides of chamise, sagebrush, yucca, and Our Lord's Candle. Just before the 2-mile point, the trail switches back several times in a slow approach to the water. The

| Lake Morena in the distance

PCT drops into a shaded oak ravine, where a spur trail comes in from the north. The bright scarlet bugler flowers are particularly stunning here, enveloping this section of the path in season.

The trail, making a gradual climb, snakes due west and crosses several jeep roads before forking left. After passing through a metal gate, you'll notice that the isolation

of this pleasant trail fades. Houses line this stretch of the PCT, which leads directly to the shoreline. In a grassy field of sagebrush, the trail splits, with the right fork leading to the water and the left going to the Lake Morena County Park campground. For those wanting to overnight, this is a good spot to camp and refuel for the next leg of the journey.

Those continuing to Morena Butte or Hauser Canyon can stock up on supplies at a nearby food store. Hikers may want to try fishing for catfish, bass, and bluegill (fishing permits are $5/day). Those planning to return to the launching point 4 miles back should pay close attention since jeep roads and fishermen's paths can lead hikers astray.

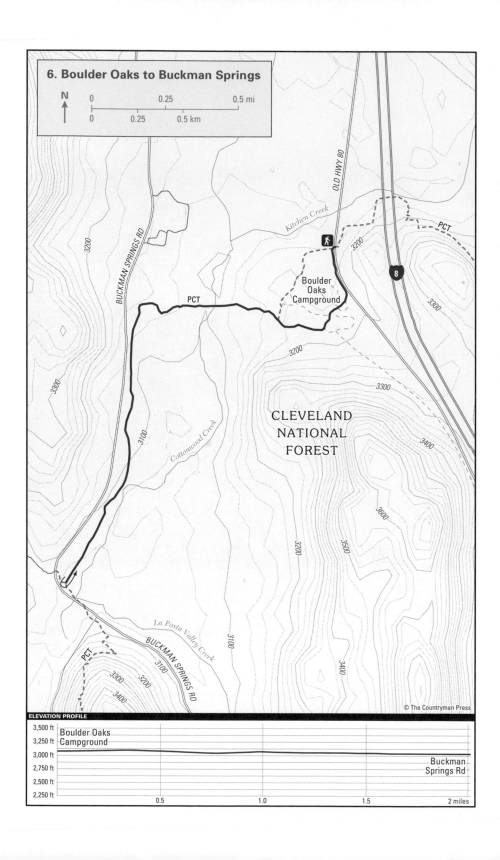

6. Boulder Oaks to Buckman Springs

N

0   0.25   0.5 mi

0   0.25   0.5 km

BUCKMAN SPRINGS RD

Kitchen Creek

OLD HWY 80

PCT

PCT

3200

3200

3300

8

Boulder
Oaks
Campground

3200

3200

3300

3100

3300

3400

Cottonwood Creek

CLEVELAND
NATIONAL
FOREST

3200

3500

3600

3400

La Posta Valley Creek

PCT

BUCKMAN SPRINGS RD

3100

3300

3200

3100

3400

3300

3400

© The Countryman Press

ELEVATION PROFILE

3,500 ft	Boulder Oaks			
3,250 ft	Campground			
3,000 ft				
2,750 ft				Buckman
2,500 ft				Springs Rd
2,250 ft				
	0.5	1.0	1.5	2 miles

Hike 6

Boulder Oaks to Buckman Springs

Distance: 4 miles round-trip

Hiking time: 1.5–2 hours

Trail highlights: Family-friendly campsite, shady oak grove, pleasant meadow

Difficulty: ▲

Family friendly: ▲ ▲

Scenery: ▲

Solitude: ▲

Trail condition: ▲ ▲ ▲

Getting There

Exit Interstate 8 onto Buckman Springs Road, and head south 2 miles on the frontage road, Old Highway 80. Just north of the PCT trailhead is a dirt turnout with space for ten cars. Additional parking is available at Boulder Oaks Campground. Vehicles must display a National Forest Adventure Pass.

| The colors of springtime. Photo by Rory Lavender.

Overview

Because of the lackluster landscape, this hike is generally made only by those on their way north to Kitchen Creek Falls or south to Lake Morena. From the paved frontage road, the level trail enters the pleasant Boulder Oaks Campground, which has horse corrals and 30 campsites. After forking onto the narrow Pacific Crest Trail, the path skirts gray boulders, atypical of the red rock formations usually found in the Laguna Mountains. Nearly half of this hike parallels Buckman Springs Road, so the sound of passing cars intrudes on the solitude and tranquility. Just beyond a shallow marsh is a meadow of live oaks. This section of the PCT ends just below a white bridge at Buckman Springs Road, the starting point for Hike 5, which leads to Lake Morena.

In Detail

This trailhead was once easy to find because of the well-known Boulder Oaks Store. The Forest Service removed it in the late 1990s after a legal battle over land use. All that remains is a small section of the foundation near the trailhead.

To begin, head south on the narrow path that parallels the frontage road just beyond the bus stop. The PCT post may be difficult to find in this grassy plain of overgrown yarrow. The marker is beneath the large power line between the parking area and the campground entrance.

After turning into Boulder Oaks Campground, continue on the wide dirt road that passes through the site. The campground is closed March through May, during the arroyo-toad breeding season. Campsites range from $14 to $32 per night and include grills, water spigots, and horse corrals.

Just beyond the corrals, the PCT narrows off to the right, passing through a metal gate and a series of boulders. From March through July, vibrant clusters of Indian paintbrush add beauty to this otherwise colorless trek.

The inviting shade of live oaks is sadly inaccessible because of a barbed-wire fence that frames the trail. After crossing a marsh, the trail briefly enters a sage grove where squirrels scurry from tree to tree.

At 1 mile, the trail parallels Buckman Springs Road for the remainder of the hike. Just beyond the auburn manzanitas is a pleasant meadow. Pass the two jeep crossings that are aromatically separated by fields of white sage and scarlet bugler.

A dip into a ravine flattens out before intersecting with an old paved road. Follow it south to the white bridge at Boulder Springs Road. A large oak provides much-needed shade on hot days. From here, hikers can return to the trailhead at Boulder Oaks or continue 4 miles south along the PCT to Lake Morena (profiled in Hike 5).

| Heading toward shade near Boulder Oaks

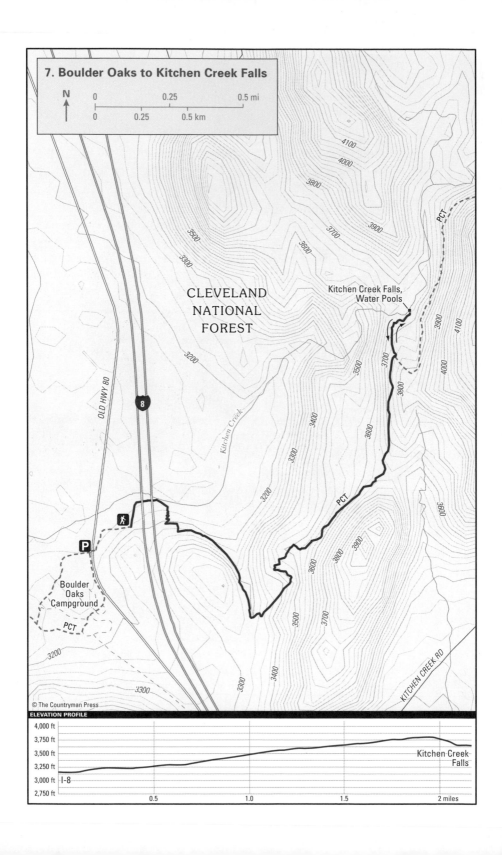

7. Boulder Oaks to Kitchen Creek Falls

N

| 0 | | 0.25 | | 0.5 mi |
| 0 | 0.25 | | 0.5 km | |

4100
4000
3800
3900
3700
3600
3500
3300

CLEVELAND
NATIONAL
FOREST

Kitchen Creek Falls,
Water Pools

3200

PCT

OLD HWY 80

8

Kitchen Creek

3400
3300
3200

3500
3700
3600
3800
3900

3600

PCT

P

Boulder
Oaks
Campground

PCT

3200

3300

3400
3500
3700
3600
3900
3800

KITCHEN CREEK RD

© The Countryman Press

ELEVATION PROFILE

4,000 ft				
3,750 ft				
3,500 ft				
3,250 ft				Kitchen Creek
3,000 ft	I-8			Falls
2,750 ft				
	0.5	1.0	1.5	2 miles

Hike 7

Boulder Oaks to Kitchen Creek Falls

Distance: 4 miles round trip	
Hiking time: 2.5 hours	
Trail highlights: Tiered cascades, canyon descent, refreshing pools	
Difficulty: ▲▲	
Family friendly: ▲▲	
Scenery: ▲▲▲	
Solitude: ▲▲	
Trail condition: ▲▲	

Getting There

Exit Interstate 8 onto Buckman Springs Road, and head south for 2 miles on the frontage road, Old Highway 80. Directly across from the trailhead is a dirt turnout with space for ten cars. Overflow parking is available just south of the trail at the Boulder Oaks Campground. Vehicles must display a National Forest Adventure Pass. To reach the trailhead, walk across the frontage road to the wide path below Interstate 8. A PCT post marks the gateway to this 4.5-mile journey.

GPS TRAILHEAD COORDINATES

UTM Zone	11S
Easting	548629
Northing	3621908
Latitude	N32.73392°
Longitude	W116.48099°

Overview

A highlight of the Laguna Mountains area, this steady climb rewards hikers with one of the few places to find cascading waterfalls in San Diego County. The winding trail improves with each step, beginning with an arid slope and peaking at a multilayered canyon ridge.

Nature's symphony, performed by croaking yellow-legged frogs, chirping birds, and the trickling waters of Kitchen Creek, quickly drowns out the bustle of Interstate 8. An adventurous descent leads to platforms of polished granite and refreshing waterfalls offering refuge in their cool waters. This turnaround point is an ideal spot to relax and indulge in a well-earned picnic. The hike is best enjoyed during winter or spring, when the creek is at its highest level. Botanists will want to visit in April, when wildflowers are in bloom.

Description

Just before a green metal gate, traffic roars overhead on elevated Interstate 8. Running parallel to the path, a canopy of oaks traces the banks of near-stagnant (at this point) Kitchen Creek. Farther on, the Pacific Crest Trail begins a slow, steady climb to the right.

The first ascent snakes several times before settling on a northeast direction. Beyond this grassy knoll, a second metal gate marks the course. Gradually, the trail

| Kitchen Creek Falls

narrows past shrub-covered slopes, spring wildflowers, and praline-colored rocks.

Farther into the climb are manzanitas, their signature auburn tones giving way to bleached hues of white and gray. Embedded in the dirt path are slabs of limestone forming steps on a natural, winding staircase. Sprouting from the edge of the trail are clusters of cane cholla cactus.

Just after the first mile, a massive boulder forces the path to bear left. Its top provides a visual recap of the PCT, but it is safer to climb the far side next to the trail than the rock face you first see.

A small cactus garden marking both sides of the trail indicates the 2-mile point. After you round the bend, a side path discreetly dips left into the Kitchen Creek Falls area. For the average hiker, this will occur approximately one hour into the trek. Generally, a cairn will mark the faint trail leading into the canyon side. For a clear view of the waterfalls from 100 feet above them, continue on the main path for another quarter mile. If you can see the waterfalls from above, you have passed the side trail to Kitchen Creek.

The descent tends to be jagged and overgrown with shrubs. When you reach the sandy creek bank, however, you see a series of cascades plummeting 150 vertical feet over granite platforms. Each platform acts as a private dock where hikers can dangle their feet in refreshing pools or bask in the sun. You may even hear the croaking of a yellow-legged frog. During the winter, the water level rises over the polished stones,

| Crossing a boulder near Kitchen Creek Falls

making the banks somewhat slippery and unpredictable.

The pools higher up Kitchen Creek are tranquil, while the faster-flowing ones downstream are more spectacular. After cooling off, head back the way you came, concluding where you began, at Old Highway 80.

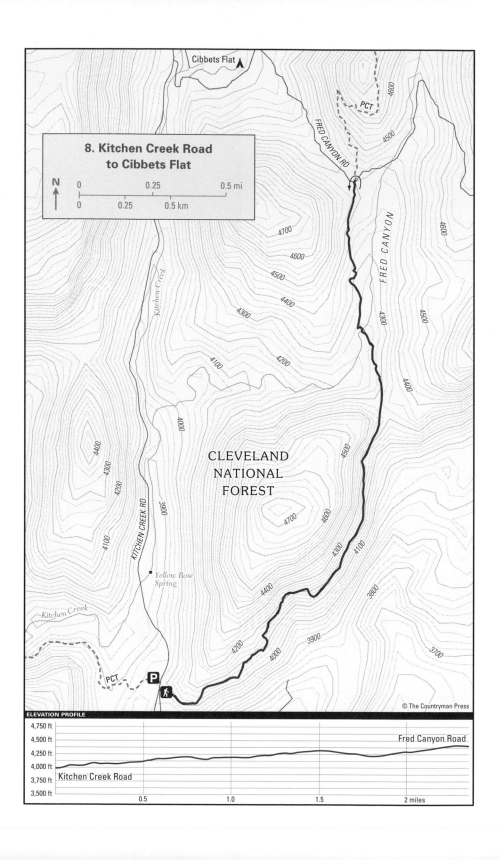

8. Kitchen Creek Road to Cibbets Flat

N

| 0 | 0.25 | 0.5 mi |
| 0 | 0.25 | 0.5 km |

Cibbets Flat

PCT

FRED CANYON RD

4600
4500

FRED CANYON

4600

4700
4600
4500
4400
4300
4200
4100

Kitchen Creek

4300
4500
4400

4000

4400
4300
4200
4100

KITCHEN CREEK RD

3900

CLEVELAND
NATIONAL
FOREST

4500

4700
4600
4300
4100

Yellow Rose
Spring

4400

Kitchen Creek

4200
4000
3900

3800

3700

PCT

P

© The Countryman Press

ELEVATION PROFILE

| 4,750 ft |
| 4,500 ft |
| 4,250 ft |
| 4,000 ft |
| 3,750 ft |
| 3,500 ft |

Fred Canyon Road

Kitchen Creek Road

0.5   1.0   1.5   2 miles

Kitchen Creek Road to Cibbets Flat

Distance: 5 miles round-trip	
Hiking time: 2.5 hours	
Trail highlights: Valley views, gneissic rock formations, glade of oaks	
Difficulty: ▲▲	
Family friendly: ▲▲	
Scenery: ▲▲	
Solitude: ▲▲	
Trail condition: ▲▲	

Getting There

Exit Interstate 8 at Kitchen Creek Road. Head north along the paved road to the first cattle guard, which is directly across from the PCT. Parking is available for approximately five cars on the side of the road. Vehicles must display a National Forest Adventure Pass. The trailhead is just east of Kitchen Creek Road.

GPS TRAILHEAD COORDINATES

UTM Zone	11S
Easting	550663
Northing	3623589
Latitude	N32.74898°
Longitude	W116.45919°

Overview

Starting at Kitchen Creek Road, this brief section of the Pacific Crest Trail offers its best views in the initial climb, which overlook Cameron Valley in the distance. A gradual ascent passes chaparral slopes lined, in season, with flowers of scarlet larkspur and Eaton's firecracker. Jutting from the hills like massive crystal formations are rust-hued gneissic rocks. After dipping into a small oak grove, the trail ascends on the west side of Fred Canyon. During springtime, this somewhat monotonous landscape is pleasantly

| Scarlet Larkspur *(Delphinium Cardinale)*

| Admiring the view of Mexico and Cameron Valley

sprinkled with the blossoms of woolly blue curls and forget-me-nots. The final moderate climb, past thick chamise shrubs, concludes at Fred Canyon Road, 0.6 miles from Cibbets Flat Campground. For those who want to extend the route, this hike can be linked to Hike 7 (Boulder Oaks to Kitchen Creek Falls) and Hike 10 (Burnt Rancheria to Cibbets Flat).

In Detail

Begin on the east side of Kitchen Creek Road, where the trail is clearly marked with a PCT post and a cattle gate. In spring, lower elevations of this hike are decorated with yellow mariposa lilies, each blossom edged in brown as if hand-dipped in chocolate.

Half a mile into the trek, gneiss rock accents the chaparral slopes. Several of these crystal-like platforms offer ideal points for taking in the view, which spans from the Mexican border to the valley below. Just before completing the first mile, the trail briefly

drops past an entire hillside covered in smooth rock slabs.

The trail continues to climb, finally leveling off around 4,300 feet. Departing from the valley ridge, it enters a thicker landscape of chaparral. A cluster of oaks offers the first and last shade on this exposed hike. After crossing a normally dry creek bed, the trail switches back west and then north along Fred Canyon. Ceanothus and chamise drape the slopes, which are seasonally colored with blue wildflowers and white sage.

Just beyond a dirt clearing, the PCT spills onto Fred Canyon Road. Occasionally, emergency water bottles can be found beneath the bushes of this wide, open space. For shade, restrooms, and water, follow the signs to Cibbets Flat Campground, half a mile northwest of the road crossing. Campsites, available year round, cost $14 per night.

Hikers can either continue north along the PCT toward Burnt Rancheria or turn back toward the trailhead at Kitchen Creek Road.

Hike 9

Cottonwood Creek Falls

Distance: 2 miles round-trip	
Hiking time: 1 hour	
Trail highlights: Swimming holes, effort-less descent, oak-shaded banks	
Difficulty: ▲	
Family friendly: ▲▲▲▲	
Scenery: ▲▲▲	
Solitude: ▲▲	
Trail condition: ▲▲▲	

GPS TRAILHEAD COORDINATES	
UTM Zone	11S
Easting	547207
Northing	3632243
Latitude	N32.82720°
Longitude	W116.49564°

Getting There

From Interstate 8, exit onto Sunrise Highway (County Road S1), and continue north for 2 miles. Between mile markers 15 and 15.5 are pullout areas on each side of Sunrise Highway. During most weekends, hikers can purchase a National Forest Adventure Pass from rangers stationed on the east side of the road. The greatest challenge of the hike is locating the trailhead, which is on the right side of the guardrail. A utility pole marks the start of the narrow, overgrown path. Be careful when crossing the road if parked in the larger lot; drivers have a tendency to speed in this area.

Overview

What this trail lacks in length, it makes up in beauty. Ideal for the less-aggressive hiker, Cottonwood Creek Falls is minutes from the Pacific Crest Trail and can be considered a downsized version of its sister trail, Kitchen Creek Falls. The 2-mile round-trip hike offers a direct path to a series of freshwater cascades. This hike is best enjoyed in winter, spring, and early summer, when the creek is still flowing; otherwise it is likely to be dry.

In Detail

Having started this trail by straddling a guardrail adjacent to a main thoroughfare, hikers may initially wonder if they are, in fact, at the trailhead. When not maintained, the dirt path is walled with overgrown trees and shrubs, forcing hikers to tunnel through uncomfortably.

After several minutes, the shaded path opens into a V-shaped trail, formerly a utility road leading to power lines. Despite the brevity of the hike, there is a wide variety of

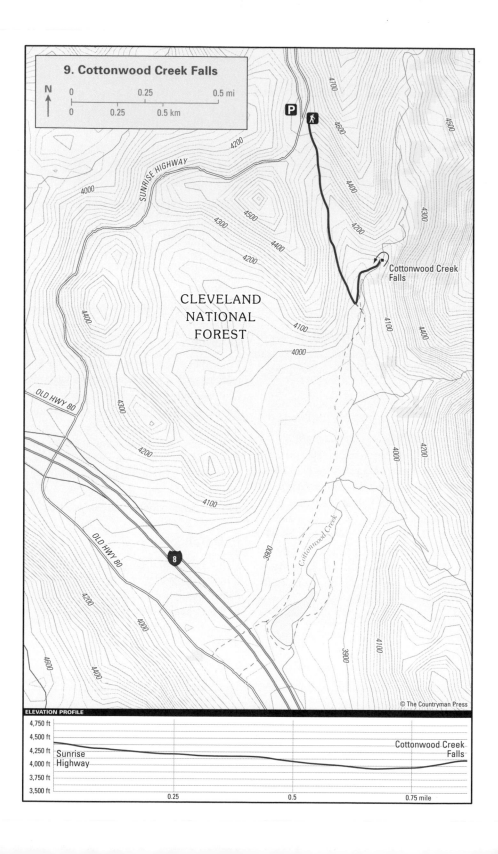

9. Cottonwood Creek Falls

N

| 0 | 0.25 | 0.5 mi |
| 0 | 0.25 | 0.5 km |

P

4700
4600
4500
4400
4300
4200
4200
4500
4300
4400
4200
4100
4100
4400
4200
4000
4000
4100
4200
4000
3900
3900
4100
4600
4400
4200
4000

SUNRISE HIGHWAY

CLEVELAND
NATIONAL
FOREST

OLD HWY 80

OLD HWY 80

8

Cottonwood Creek
Falls

Cottonwood Creek

© The Countryman Press

ELEVATION PROFILE

4,750 ft			
4,500 ft			
4,250 ft	Sunrise		Cottonwood Creek
4,000 ft	Highway		Falls
3,750 ft			
3,500 ft	0.25	0.5	0.75 mile

| Cottonwood Creek Falls

plant life, including Spanish bayonet, yucca, and white ceanothus.

The path becomes a loose walkway of multicolored stones and pebbles. In spring, fields of dry brush fade into a colorful backdrop of woolly blue curls and lavender beardtongue. At the bottom of the descent, about 3/4 of a mile down, the road forks at a field of perennial bunchgrass. Take a sharp left and walk upstream along Cottonwood Creek, keeping the water to your right.

Follow the path through the tree graveyard, where a cluster of fallen oaks form piles of tangled limbs among new growth. You can lunch here and enjoy the babbling creek, which warms in May. Make your way to the clear pools; the deepest is about 5-feet when water levels are high. Sheets of water gush over rock platforms to create the cascades.

Leading to the top tier of the cascades is a rust-toned boulder pathway, beautifully framed by red-berry shrubs and prickly pear cactus. The creek dries to a trickle by early summer, making December through May the best time to visit the falls.

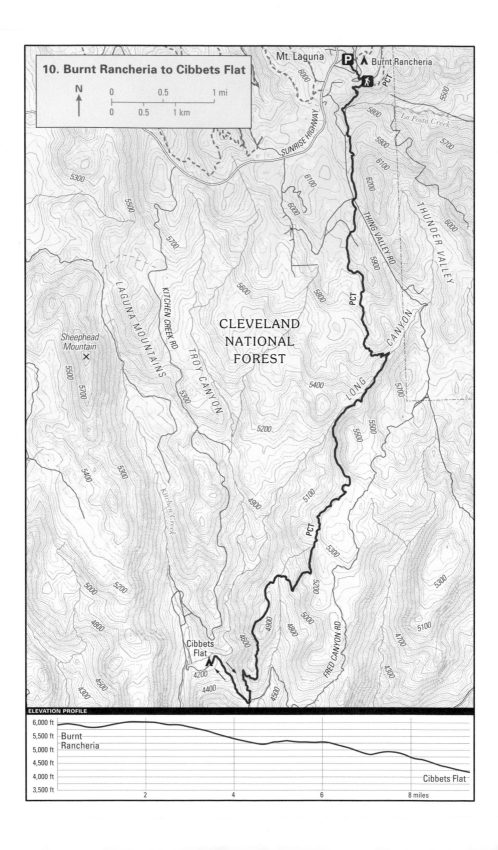

10. Burnt Rancheria to Cibbets Flat

N

0   0.5   1 mi
0   0.5   1 km

Mt. Laguna

P ⋏ Burnt Rancheria

PCT

La Posta Creek

SUNRISE HIGHWAY

THING VALLEY RD

THUNDER VALLEY

LONG CANYON

PCT

CLEVELAND
NATIONAL
FOREST

LAGUNA MOUNTAINS

KITCHEN CREEK RD

TROY CANYON

Sheephead
Mountain
×

Kitchen Creek

PCT

FRED CANYON RD

Cibbets
Flat ⋏

ELEVATION PROFILE

6,000 ft
5,500 ft   Burnt
5,000 ft   Rancheria
4,500 ft
4,000 ft   Cibbets Flat
3,500 ft

        2   4   6   8 miles

Hike 10

Burnt Rancheria to Cibbets Flat

Distance: 20 miles round-trip		
Hiking time: 9 hours		
Trail highlights: Piñon pines, trickling stream, dramatic landscape, campsite		
Difficulty: ▲▲▲		
Family friendly: ▲		
Scenery: ▲▲▲		
Solitude: ▲▲▲		
Trail condition: ▲▲▲		

GPS TRAILHEAD COORDINATES

UTM Zone	11S
Easting	554439
Northing	3635743
Latitude	N32.85843°
Longitude	W116.41817°

Getting There

Exit Interstate 8 onto Sunrise Highway (County Road S1), and continue for approximately 10 miles to mile marker 22.5. Turn right into Burnt Rancheria Campground and park toward the back near the amphitheater. The 20-car parking area offers public restrooms beside the trailhead sign reading NATURE TRAIL. Be sure to display a National Forest Adventure Pass. To reserve a campsite at Burnt Rancheria Campground ($20/night), call 619-473-0120 or 619-445-6235.

To complete the hike in reverse, Cibbets Flat Campground (the midway point for this hike) can be reached from Interstate 8 by exiting at Kitchen Creek Road and heading north for 4.5 miles. Twenty-five campsites are available at Cibbets Flat, starting at $14. For more information, contact 619-445-6235.

Overview

In the late 1800s, cattlemen invaded the Lagunas ("lakes") Mountains, which were inhabited by the Kumeyaay Native Americans. In protest, the natives burned the ranch house; hence the name Burnt Rancheria. Today the area is a popular campground for families. Built in 1960 and renovated in 2006, it offers everything from a forest amphitheater to private fire pits.

The two campgrounds—Burnt Rancheria and Cibbets Flat—on either end of this trail make the 20-mile hike (round-trip) a perfect way to spend the weekend. Beginning at Burnt Rancheria Campground, the trail meanders past picnic areas, water spigots, fire pits, and restrooms. Open mid-April through October, the campground offers summer children's activities and campfire programs for families. After passing through these tailored grounds, the path drops away from the Desert View Trail and joins the PCT.

Piñon pine and black oak abound in this area, adding lushness and shade as the trail begins to descend. With Thunder Valley to the east, the route passes along shaded La Posta Creek and gradually drops toward Long Canyon. Switchbacks and saddle crossings give way to breathtaking views of Horse Meadow, the Laguna Mountains, and Lake Morena to the south. The reward of this hike is resting (or overnighting) at Cibbets Flat Campground.

In Detail

Begin at the trailhead for the Desert View Trail at the far end of the campground beside the amphitheater. Follow the numbered posts marked "Laguna Mountain Recreation Area." Each post marks a stop on the summer nature tours where guides explain a fact about the landscape and flora. Campfire programs, children's activities, and free guided hikes are available during summer months. Schedules can be obtained at the Visitor Information Center or by calling 619-473-8547.

In the first stretch of trail, the dirt path will cross several paved roads leading to designated campsites. Shading the picnic area are black oaks sprouting leafy mistletoe. At the 0.2-mile point, drop away from the Desert View Trail, and head south (right) onto the PCT. The route dips into shaded forest where wild lilac and Jeffrey pine perfume the air with the sweet scent of vanilla. This section is particularly stunning because of the piñon pines, which are generally more prevalent on the desert slopes of Riverside County. These stately trees produce pine nuts, once popular with the Kumeyaays, who roasted and ground the nuts with sage and chia seeds.

Dark mountain mahogany, a member of the rose family, dots this cool segment of the trail. In the spring, purple beardtongue, Canadian thistle, and lavender lupine thrive in the shadows of the trees. Echoing high above is the sound of woodpeckers chiseling holes into the trunks of Jeffrey pines. Directly east is Thunder Valley. Here the trail switches back several times before paralleling Thing Valley Road.

Cross the old jeep road and ascend a small slope, where western wallflowers, Indian paintbrush, and checkerblooms line the path in springtime. Wooden signs in a wide clearing list the distances to Fred Canyon Road and Boulder Oaks, farther south on the PCT.

Clusters of boulders and bushes of ceanothus mark the gateway to Long Canyon. Here the scenery transforms, as forest yields to slopes of yucca, chamise, and manzanita. After crossing La Posta Creek, hikers are often treated to the sound of trickling water and the coolness of a shaded trail, which briefly reenters forest territory. Marking the final entrance into arid landscape are Our Lord's Candle towering from the hillsides. They are especially beautiful in May and June, when they flower.

Here the trail drops southeast, switching back numerous times until it parallels the creek. Sage-covered hills roll toward paved Kitchen Creek Road in the distance. Multiple twists and turns give way to breathtaking views of Lake Morena to the south. Cradled deep in the belly of Fred Canyon is the secluded Cibbets Flat Campground. Leave the PCT and break away to the right. Follow the dirt road 0.8 miles west toward the campground, which is equipped with tables, restrooms, grills, and water. Although the grounds are open year-round, reservations must be made four days in advance.

Turn around to complete the hike by returning to the Desert View Trail trailhead at Burnt Rancheria Campground.

Continuing south on the PCT takes you to Kitchen Creek Road (Hike 8) and eventually to Boulder Oaks, past Kitchen Creek Falls (Hike 7).

| Hiking from Burnt Rancheria to Cibbets Flat

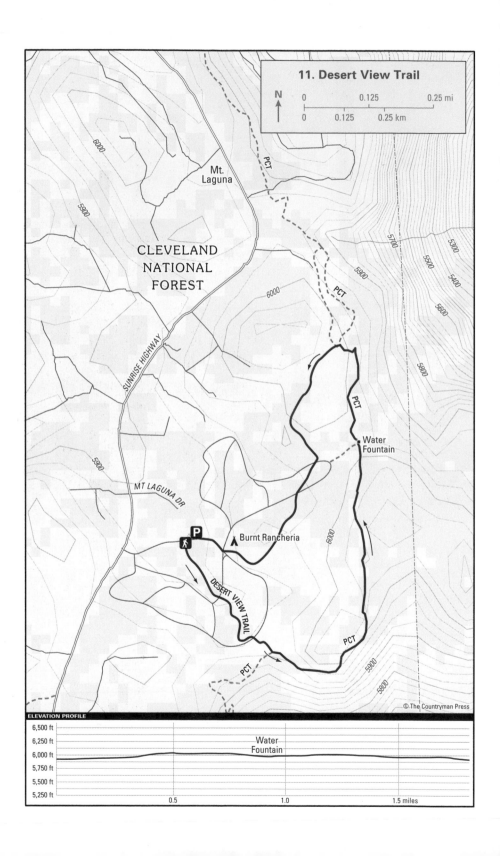

11. Desert View Trail

N

| 0 | 0.125 | | 0.25 mi |
| 0 | 0.125 | 0.25 km | |

Mt.
Laguna

PCT

6000

5300

5700

5900

5300

5500

5400

5600

CLEVELAND
NATIONAL
FOREST

6000

PCT

5800

PCT

Water
Fountain

SUNRISE HIGHWAY

5900

MT LAGUNA DR

6000

P

Burnt Rancheria

PCT

DESERT VIEW TRAIL

5900

PCT

PCT

5800

© The Countryman Press

ELEVATION PROFILE

| 6,500 ft |
| 6,250 ft |
| 6,000 ft |
| 5,750 ft |
| 5,500 ft |
| 5,250 ft |

Water
Fountain

0.5   1.0   1.5 miles

Hike 11
Desert View Trail

Distance: 1.3 mile loop

Hiking time: 1 hour

Trail highlights: Picnic areas, optional offshoot trail, desert views

Difficulty: ▲

Family friendly: ▲▲▲▲

Scenery: ▲▲▲

Solitude: ▲

Trail condition: ▲▲▲

Getting There

Exit Interstate 8 onto Sunrise Highway (County Road S1), and continue approximately 10 miles to mile marker 22.5. Turn right into Burnt Rancheria Campground, and park toward the back near the amphitheater. The 20-car parking area offers public restrooms beside the trailhead sign reading "Nature Trail." National Forest Adventure Passes must be displayed on vehicles parked in this area. To reserve a campsite at Burnt Rancheria Campground ($20/night), call 619-473-0120 or 619-445-6235.

GPS TRAILHEAD COORDINATES	
UTM Zone	11S
Easting	554908
Northing	3636679
Latitude	N32.86685°
Longitude	W116.41311°

Overview

The well-groomed starting point of Desert View Trail is the first indication that the hike is going to be a pleasant one. Skirting Burnt Rancheria Campground, the trail meanders through a storybook forest of oak and pine before connecting to the PCT. After traversing a ridge, the hiker is treated to spectacular views of neighboring canyons and the Anza-Borrego Desert. Hikers can either

| A shady spot on the Desert View Trail

loop back to the trailhead or briefly continue north on the PCT for bonus views with minimal effort. With 260 feet in elevation gain, this brief hike takes about an hour, making it ideal for families with small children.

In Detail

From the trailhead, pass the amphitheater on your left and continue straight along the dirt path. In the first few minutes, the trail will cross three paved paths that lead to various sections of Burnt Rancheria Campground. Numbered posts mark the journey through a peaceful Jeffrey-pine forest dotted by shaded picnic areas.

At a quarter mile, the Desert View Trail merges with the PCT. Head north (left) for a dramatic change in scenery. The gradual climb follows a rocky ridge lined with prickly pear cactus, chaparral, and other desert plants. In late winter, golden leaves are visible in the distant forest.

The steeper ascent gives way to jagged boulders that seem to melt into the trail, often overtaking it with red-rock pavement. Adding hints of diversity to the terrain are manzanita trees and California mugwort, an herb traditionally used by Native Americans for colds, bronchitis, asthma, and skin wounds.

After briefly paralleling a barbed-wire fence, the trail comes to a large clearing with a stone water fountain. Continue north, where cactus clusters and purple-hued chaparral blanket the hills. Views of the Laguna Mountains and the Anza-Borrego Desert begin here.

The Desert View Trail continues to the left, looping back to the campground. (For even more exceptional views, continue briefly north on the PCT toward the radar domes. To avoid a tiring climb back to the Desert View Trail, try dipping into the PCT

| Jagged boulders on Desert View Trail

for roughly a quarter of a mile. The initial mountainous views offer a taste of what lies ahead. Continuing north on the PCT can be addictive, however, because of the breathtaking views around every bend.)

Back on the loop, just beyond the PCT–

Desert View Trail split, a grassy knoll and an enormous oak provide an ideal resting point. The trail's final stretch descends through thick forest along a pine-needled path, finally returning at the campground where the hike began.

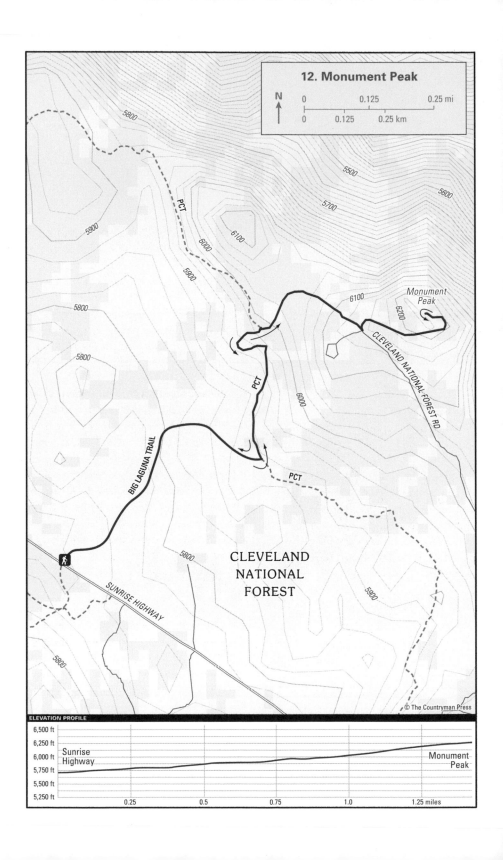

12. Monument Peak

N
0   0.125   0.25 mi
0   0.125   0.25 km

5800

PCT

5500

5700

5600

5900

6000

6100

Monument
Peak

6100

6200

5800

CLEVELAND NATIONAL FOREST RD

5800

PCT

6000

BIG LAGUNA TRAIL

PCT

5800

CLEVELAND
NATIONAL
FOREST

5900

SUNRISE HIGHWAY

5900

5900

© The Countryman Press

ELEVATION PROFILE

6,500 ft					
6,250 ft					
6,000 ft	Sunrise				Monument
5,750 ft	Highway				Peak
5,500 ft					
5,250 ft					
	0.25	0.5	0.75	1.0	1.25 miles

Hike 12

Monument Peak

Distance: 3 miles round-trip	
Hiking time: 1.5 hours	
Trail highlights: Pine forest, summit at turnaround, wide-ranging views	
Difficulty: ▲	
Family friendly: ▲▲▲	
Scenery: ▲▲▲	
Solitude: ▲▲	
Trail condition: ▲▲▲	

Getting There

Exit Interstate 8 onto Sunrise Highway (County Road S1). Drive 12.5 miles to mile marker 25.2 on Sunrise Highway. Park in the dirt turnout area, where a large stump dots the center of the eight-car space. The trailhead, labeled "Big Laguna Trail," leads directly off the parking area and into a beautiful pine forest. All vehicles parked in this area must display a National Forest Adventure Pass.

GPS TRAILHEAD COORDINATES

UTM Zone	11S
Easting	553707
Northing	3639018
Latitude	N32.88801°
Longitude	W116.42580°

Overview

While the Pacific Crest Trail may be known for its taxing terrain, the Monument Peak Trail is inviting because of its short length and its simplicity. It traverses the Laguna Mountain ridgeline, offering sweeping views of the Anza Borrego Desert. Since this hike is brief and relatively easy, those who want more of a challenge should combine it with neighboring hikes such as Garnet Peak (profiled in Hike 17).

Meandering past thick chaparral and pine woods, the trail connects to the PCT and begins a gradual ascent. Eventually it splits off into a manzanita field, where clusters of auburn branches form perfect domes, like mushroom tops. Although the climb is somewhat lackluster, the summit views make this trail worth the effort. On a very clear day, hikers can see across the desert, all the way to the Salton Sea and Chocolate Mountains.

In Detail

From the parking area, the narrow dirt path marked "Big Laguna Trail" enters a forest of chamise, high scrub, Jeffrey pine, and black oak. Trunks and branches bored by armies of termites lie scattered in brittle mounds. Pine needles and cones form a blanket over the trail.

| Desert floor of Anza-Borrego

At the half-mile mark, turn left onto the PCT and continue along its gradual grade. Shaded by Jeffrey pines, the trail bends left through a series of red rock formations and manzanita trees.

At the fork, head right rather than following the PCT to the left. Head toward the communication antenna that juts out from Monument Peak. Unfortunately, this blot on the landscape is the key point of reference on this hike. Lavender chaparral and mountain mahogany form thick brush walls on both sides of the rocky trail. This most strenuous section of the hike is rather brief.

Just before reaching the top of the hill, be sure to gaze back at the stunning view behind you. The trail will eventually reach a fenced-in laser-research facility. Walk along the fence toward the paved road on the left. As you approach the antenna, focus on the spectacular views to the east. The desert floor of Anza-Borrego dramatically scoops the base of the Laguna and Sawtooth Mountains.

When returning, be careful not to pass the turnoff point back to the trailhead. Look for two PCT posts marking both sides of the Big Laguna Trail entrance.

Hike 13

Foster Point

Distance: 1.3 miles round-trip	
Hiking time: 1 hour	
Trail highlights: Forest trail, well-marked terrain, mapping monument	
Difficulty: ▲	
Family friendly: ▲▲▲▲	
Scenery: ▲▲	
Solitude: ▲▲	
Trail condition: ▲▲▲	

Getting There

Exit Interstate 8 onto Sunrise Highway (CR S1), and continue to mile marker 25.7. Park opposite Horse Heaven Group Campground, where an old dirt road swings east toward the PCT. On the east side of Sunrise Highway, there is parking for approximately five cars. Additional parking is available across the road at the campground entrance. Vehicles must display a National Forest Adventure Pass.

GPS TRAILHEAD COORDINATES

UTM Zone	11S
Easting	552304
Northing	3639154
Latitude	N32.88930°
Longitude	W116.44080°

Overview

Among Laguna's short hikes, Foster Point offers one of the most outstanding views with the least amount of effort. Branching off from Sunrise Highway (County Road S1), a marked trail splits through a peaceful forest of pine and oak. Changing suddenly as if it were a pull-down backdrop, the scenery becomes a manzanita labyrinth climbing toward Foster's summit. The panoramic highlights of this jaunt are conveniently mapped out on a direction finder at the turnaround point.

| The trail to Foster's Point

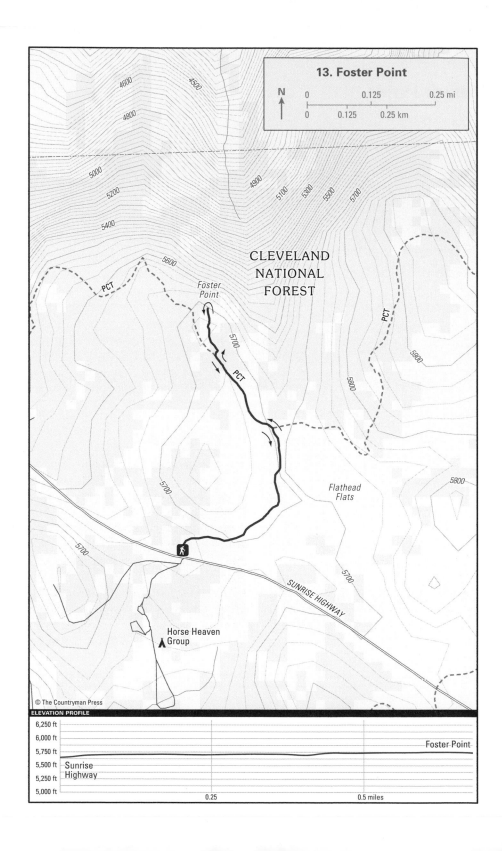

13. Foster Point

N

| 0 | 0.125 | 0.25 mi |

| 0 | 0.125 | 0.25 km |

4600

4800

4500

5000

4900

5100

5300

5500

5700

5200

5400

5600

PCT

Foster
Point

5700

PCT

CLEVELAND
NATIONAL
FOREST

PCT

5900

5800

5700

Flathead
Flats

5800

5700

5700

5700

SUNRISE HIGHWAY

Horse Heaven
Group

© The Countryman Press

ELEVATION PROFILE

6,250 ft			
6,000 ft			
5,750 ft			Foster Point
5,500 ft	Sunrise		
5,250 ft	Highway		
5,000 ft		0.25	0.5 miles

| View of Sawtooth and San Gorgonio Mountains

In Detail

From Sunrise Highway, walk east along the service road strewn with chopped trees and stumpy logs. The trail enters a staggered forest of pine and oak known as Flathead Flats. Chamise shrubs bloom from branches that fan slightly over the trail's edge.

At 0.3 mile, the dirt road connects to the Pacific Crest Trail, which climbs north (left) through a chaparral ravine. As it departs from woodland scenery, the trail passes several Jeffrey pines before entering a field of wild brush. Thick manzanitas frame the trail,

their auburn branches shaded by leafy caps.

After 0.2 mile on the PCT, follow the wooden sign pointing toward Foster Point. At the final 100-yard climb, a waist-high labyrinth of manzanita seems almost deliberately sculpted. The last stretch is a stone trail, beautifully constructed by members of the California Sierra Club.

The turnaround point is marked by a direction finder identifying 17 peaks, including some in the Sawtooth and San Gorgonio mountains. Toward the north, the horizon seems to ripple to infinity.

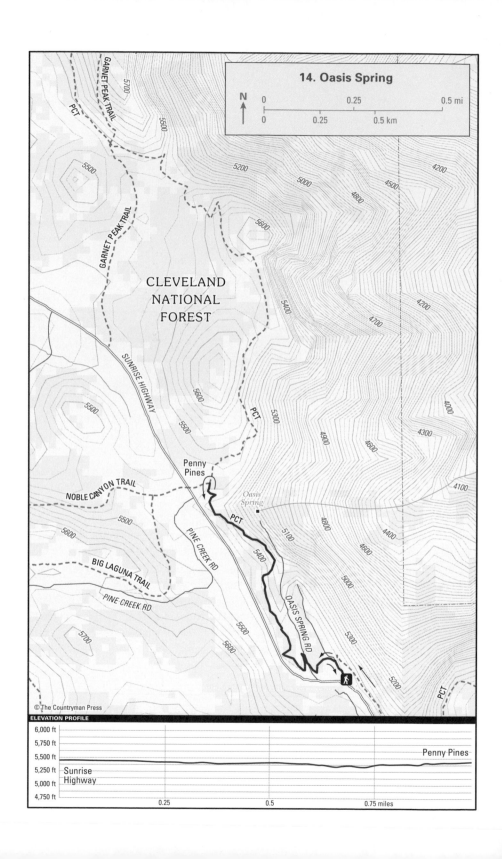

14. Oasis Spring

N

| 0 | | 0.25 | | 0.5 mi |
| 0 | 0.25 | | 0.5 km | |

GARNET PEAK TRAIL

PCT

5700

5500

5500

GARNET PEAK TRAIL

5200

5000

4800

4500

4200

5600

CLEVELAND
NATIONAL
FOREST

SUNRISE HIGHWAY

5400

4700

4200

5500

5600

PCT

5300

4900

4600

4000

4300

Penny
Pines

NOBLE CANYON TRAIL

PCT

*Oasis
Spring*

4800

4100

5500

5500

5100

5400

4600

4400

5600

BIG LAGUNA TRAIL

PINE CREEK RD.

5000

PINE CREEK RD.

5300

5700

5500

OASIS SPRING RD.

5200

5600

PCT

© The Countryman Press

ELEVATION PROFILE

6,000 ft				
5,750 ft				
5,500 ft				Penny Pines
5,250 ft	Sunrise			
5,000 ft	Highway			
4,750 ft		0.25	0.5	0.75 miles

Hike 14
Oasis Spring

Distance: 2 miles round-trip
Hiking time: 1 hour
Trail highlights: Bubbling spring, shaded trail, canyon view, lush vegetation
Difficulty: ▲
Family friendly: ▲▲
Scenery: ▲▲
Solitude: ▲
Trail condition: ▲▲▲

Getting There

Exit Interstate 8 onto Sunrise Highway (CR S1) and continue north. Although many hikers access Oasis Spring through the gate at mile 26.7, there is no parking there. We recommend beginning at mile 26.5, where you can park and then find the unmarked trailhead on the east side of Sunrise Highway. A National Forest Adventure Pass is required in this area.

| Barren trees creating a natural tunnel over the trail

| Views near Oasis Spring

GPS TRAILHEAD COORDINATES

UTM Zone	11S
Easting	551447
Northing	3640041
Latitude	N32.89735°
Longitude	W116.44990°

Overview

Nestled in the Laguna Mountains, the natural splendor of Oasis Spring makes this trail inviting. The sounds of Sunset Highway gradually yield to those of the babbling brook, desert winds, and chirping birds. Around nearly every bend is another visual treasure, from maple trees to mountain mahogany. Keep in mind that Oasis Spring is usually dry by March. Sandwiched between Garnet Peak and Foster Point, this two-mile trek offers spectacular views of Storm Canyon's abyss.

In Detail

Begin at the unmarked trailhead, and proceed north along the narrow, pine-needled path. On reaching the Pacific Crest Trail, gradually ascend to the left before the trail merges with Oasis Spring Road. To the left, a metal gate leads to a trail that heads back toward Sunrise Highway (County Road S1), while the right trail snakes down a shaded ravine. Take the right option toward peaceful Oasis Spring, where lush switchbacks pass through black oak, mountain mahogany, and Jeffrey pine.

The PCT crosses the usually trickling stream from Oasis Spring. Tiers of fallen branches have conveniently created miniature cascades along the waterway. After briefly paralleling the highway, the trail curves downstream and then begins to climb Mount Laguna's ridge.

Departing from the shaded ravine, the trail becomes embedded with red stones and rock slabs, which occasionally blanket the entire path. Traverse the trail rim, keeping the canyon to the right. At one point, a cluster of arched manzanitas forms a natural tunnel over the path. At the 1-mile mark, the PCT merges with the Garnet Peak Trail, signifying the turnaround point for the Oasis Spring hike. For a bigger challenge, continue toward Garnet Peak (see Hike 17).

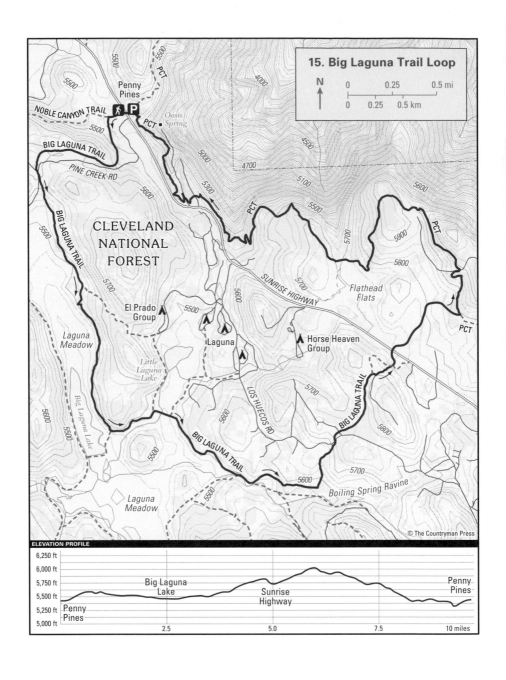

15. Big Laguna Trail Loop

N

| 0 | 0.25 | 0.5 mi |

| 0 | 0.25 | 0.5 km |

5500

5300

PCT

Penny Pines

P

Oasis Spring

NOBLE CANYON TRAIL

PCT

5500

4000

4700

5000

5300

4500

5100

BIG LAGUNA TRAIL

PINE CREEK RD

5600

5600

PCT

5500

BIG LAGUNA TRAIL

5500

CLEVELAND NATIONAL FOREST

5700

5700

5900

PCT

5800

El Prado Group

5500

Laguna Meadow

SUNRISE HIGHWAY

5600

Flathead Flats

PCT

Little Laguna Lake

Laguna

Horse Heaven Group

5700

Big Laguna Lake

5600

LOS HUECOS RD

5700

5600

BIG LAGUNA TRAIL

5600

5800

5500

BIG LAGUNA TRAIL

5600

5700

Boiling Spring Ravine

Laguna Meadow

5500

© The Countryman Press

ELEVATION PROFILE

| 6,250 ft |
| 6,000 ft |
| 5,750 ft |
| 5,500 ft |
| 5,250 ft |
| 5,000 ft |

Big Laguna Lake

Sunrise Highway

Penny Pines

Penny Pines

| 2.5 | 5.0 | 7.5 | 10 miles |

Hike 15

Big Laguna Trail Loop

Distance: 10 mile loop	
Hiking time: 5.5 hours	
Trail highlights: Quiet meadows, water views, old-growth forest, spring flowers	
Difficulty: ▲ ▲ ▲	
Family friendly: ▲	
Scenery: ▲ ▲ ▲	
Solitude: ▲ ▲	
Trail condition: ▲ ▲ ▲	

GPS TRAILHEAD COORDINATES

UTM Zone	11S
Easting	551165
Northing	3640142
Latitude	N32.89827°
Longitude	W116.45292°

Getting There

Exit Interstate 8 onto Sunrise Highway (CR S1), and continue 14 miles north to the trailhead for the Penny Pines Trail at mile marker 27.3. Approximately ten parking spots are available on the shoulder of Sunrise Highway. Hikers must display a National Forest Adventure Pass to park here. On most weekends, day passes are available at the Cottonwood Creek Falls parking area between miles 15.3 and 15.4 on Sunrise Highway.

You may see quite a few cars parked at the trailhead, but many of the hikers are probably on other nearby trails that branch off from this starting point. A large wooden sign with "Noble Canyon Trail" in yellow lettering marks the trailhead for the Big Laguna Trail. Note: They both start at the same trailhead, but then the trails split just past the launching point.

Overview

This 10-mile loop—combining 6 miles on the Big Laguna Trail with 4 miles on the PCT— is a must-do for Southern California hikers with time and motivation. The relatively flat route dishes up magnificent visions from fields laden with wildflowers to lakes providing refuge for waterfowl. After a brief stroll through pine and oak forest, the path heads toward Big Laguna Lake. In the spring, trailside slopes come alive with yellow violets and baby blue eyes.

Just before the midway point, the observant hiker may glimpse turkeys, woodpeckers, blue jays, lizards, and hawks. During the final miles, the views dramatically change from tranquil meadows to rugged terrain. No matter your preference, the Big Laguna Trail offers a slice of scenery for any hiker.

The first few miles of the Big Laguna Trail tend to get congested since bikers, horses, dogs, and hikers frequent this area. Just beyond the lake, however, the trek becomes less populated when mountain bikers fade onto spur trails because they're prohibited from the PCT.

| Big Laguna Lake

In late winter, be sure to bring a wind-breaker and waterproof hiking boots. Sheets of snow often blanket the shaded trail. The ideal months for this splendid journey are April and May, when seasonal flowers are in bloom.

In Detail

From the hike's beginning at Noble Canyon, briefly head west before turning left onto the Big Laguna Trail. This marked trail passes through a metal gate and toward the first of many contrasting backdrops. Slopes of chaparral give way to oak and pine trees, many of them over 200 years old. Some of the barren branches cluster in teardrop formations, shaped by the prevailing Santa Ana winds.

The now-minimal scars of past wildfires are almost as intriguing as the new life that stands beside them. Like charcoal pencils mounted in the ground, the charred trunks of several wounded pines stand in isolation. The wind often funnels through this forest, making it an ideal spot to view hawks soaring above.

Continue south on the Big Laguna Trail toward the meadowlands. The sounds of chirping birds and whistling winds can be heard from the branches overhead. Just after the first mile, Big Laguna Lake becomes visible on the horizon. In late winter and early spring, its pool of rainwater is at its highest.

Framing the grass plains is a thick pine forest that abruptly ends where the wind-blown meadow begins. Bordering the dirt trail are pines and patches of moss, emerald from seasonal rains and shade. Continue south (straight) on the Big Laguna Trail rather than forking toward the Prado Campground.

Eventually the trail gives way to a clear water view; you may even see horses drinking from the water's edge. Just before reaching the water, the trail bends east (left). The grassy fields reward hikers with such wildflowers as baby blue eyes, yellow violets, centauries, white yarrows, and prickly pear cacti.

Instead of passing through the fence at the end of this stretch, take a sharp right and continue hiking parallel to the barbed wire. Darting lizards and bright dandelions bring life to this segment. The power lines that drape over the purple chaparral are the sole eyesore of this picturesque journey. A second opening in the fence leads to Laguna Campground, where facilities are available.

The trail delivers its most strenuous section during the east, and then northbound, ascent toward the intersecting Los Huecos Road.

Cross over this old road to reconnect with the trail. Wild turkeys and woodpeckers can often be seen and heard here. An 80-foot pine near the 4.5-mile point is freckled with thousands of woodpecker boreholes, each of them filled with squirrel-delivered acorns. To the left of the trail, a wooden bench provides an ideal place to observe wild turkeys.

Pass through the fence, and follow the traffic sounds to Sunrise Highway (County Road S1), which the Big Laguna Trail crosses. After the highway, continue eastward for another mile to the PCT. Turn left at the PCT post to see yet another dramatic change in scenery. Sun-bleached branches, red rocks, Jeffrey pines, and black oaks dominate the landscape, giving way to the first glimpse of mountain and desert views.

Continue on the PCT through slopes of braided manzanita and California mugwort. Pause to soak in vistas of the Laguna Mountains, Anza-Borrego Desert, and the distant Salton Sea. This lookout point is just after the red boulder formations high above the right side of the trail.

The path then begins to descend, passing several other lookout spots and the popular Foster Trail. After crossing an old wooden bridge, the trail reaches Oasis Spring, which is generally dry by early March. Follow the PCT along the abrupt face of the escarpment, overlooking the desert below. To complete the hike, leave the PCT and head toward the Penny Pines parking area, where the trek began.

| Pine forest near Big Laguna Lake

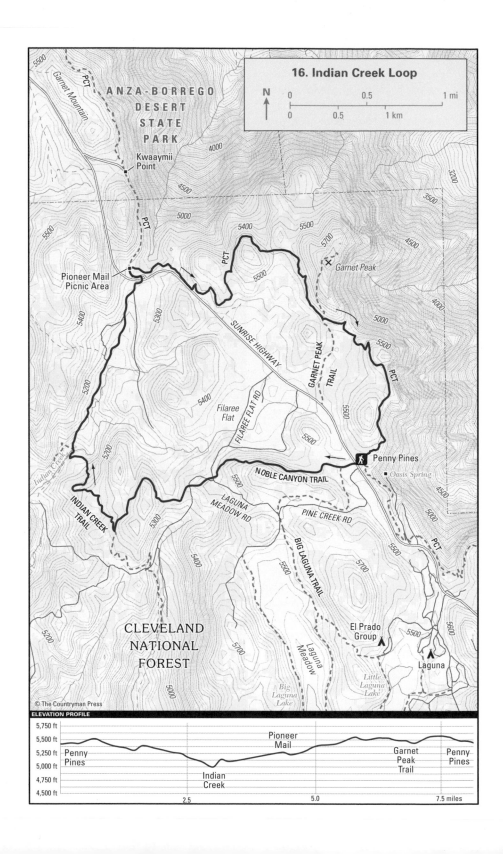

16. Indian Creek Loop

N

| 0 | | 0.5 | | 1 mi |

| 0 | 0.5 | | 1 km | |

ANZA-BORREGO
DESERT
STATE
PARK

Garnet Mountain

PCT

5500

Kwaaymii
Point

4000

4500

5000

5400

5500

5700

Garnet Peak

3200

3500

4500

4000

PCT

Pioneer Mail
Picnic Area

5500

5500

5400

5300

5200

SUNRISE HIGHWAY

5500

GARNET PEAK TRAIL

5500

5000

5500

PCT

5200

Filaree
Flat

5400

FILAREE FLAT RD

5500

5500

Penny Pines

Oasis Spring

4500

Indian Creek

5200

5300

NOBLE CANYON TRAIL

5500

PINE CREEK RD

5000

PCT

INDIAN CREEK TRAIL

5300

LAGUNA
MEADOW RD

5500

BIG LAGUNA TRAIL

5700

5600

5400

5700

5500

El Prado
Group

5500

Laguna

CLEVELAND
NATIONAL
FOREST

5200

5000

Laguna
Meadow

Little
Laguna
Lake

Big
Laguna
Lake

© The Countryman Press

ELEVATION PROFILE

5,750 ft		Pioneer		
5,500 ft		Mail		
5,250 ft	Penny		Garnet	Penny
5,000 ft	Pines		Peak	Pines
4,750 ft		Indian	Trail	
4,500 ft		Creek		

2.5   5.0   7.5 miles

Hike 16
Indian Creek Loop

Distance: 8-mile loop	
Hiking time: 4 hours	
Trail highlights: Trickling creek, canyon view, grassy knoll, blending trails	
Difficulty: ▲▲▲	
Family friendly: ▲▲	
Scenery: ▲▲▲	
Solitude: ▲▲▲	
Trail condition: ▲▲▲	

Getting There

Exit Interstate 8 onto Sunrise Highway (CR S1), and continue north to the trailhead for the Penny Pines Trail at mile marker 27.3. Ample parking is available on both shoulders. Hikers must display a National Forest Adventure Pass, available most weekends at the Cottonwood Creek Falls parking area between miles 15.3 and 15.4 on Sunrise Highway. A large wooden sign with "Noble Canyon Trail" in yellow lettering marks the trailhead. This is also the trailhead for Big Laguna Loop (see Hike 15).

GPS TRAILHEAD COORDINATES	
UTM Zone	11S
Easting	550757
Northing	3640921
Latitude	N32.90531°
Longitude	W116.45724°

Overview

In contrast to many "there-and-back" trails, the Indian Creek Loop offers breathtaking sights at every step. Setting off from Noble Canyon Trail, the path crosses a forest of oak and pine where trees show signs of lush recovery after past wildfires. Fluctuating between barren and bountiful, the landscape dramatically alters around every bend.

| Sun-bleached manzanitas

| Signs of past wildfires

Midway into the journey, after switching to the Indian Creek Trail, hikers are rewarded with the trickling waters of Indian Creek, cradled in the lap of a grassy meadow. The Indian Creek Trail then unites with the Pacific Crest Trail. Saving the best for last, the PCT portion of the trek takes hikers along the rim of Storm Canyon, bathed in pink wallflowers and valleys of lilacs in springtime.

Although blooming in beauty March through June, the Indian Creek Loop can also be enjoyed during the winter. In January and February, snow drapes the shaded woodlands split by the meandering trail. This northern section of the Laguna Mountain Recreational Area can get crowded on weekends since bikes are permitted on the trail, other than when it meets the PCT.

In Detail

To begin, follow the Noble Canyon Trail from the trailhead for the Penny Pines Trail along the dirt path heading west. A forest of thick chaparral, Jeffrey pines, and black oaks envelops the trail. Sections of the forest remain bald from the 2002 and 2003 wildfires, while others flourish with the fresh scents of resin and vanilla-like sweetness. This area was hit especially hard during the 2003 Cedar Fire that destroyed 280,278 acres.

A northbound incline offers a fuller view of the pine valley. Dropping slightly, the trail bends left, passing a cluster of boulders on the edge of a grassy ridge. Marking the completion of the first mile is a small junction. Cross over and continue past the archery hunting area. Archery season runs from September 1 through October 15 and again from November 18 through December 31. Hikers are encouraged to wear orange during hunting season. The trail will intersect a paved road several times.

As the path narrows, the terrain changes frequently. Packed earth evolves into crumbly sediment and eventually into rocks.

At 2.3 miles, the trail forks left to Pine

| Remnants of winter

Valley and right to Indian Creek Trail. Follow the posts along Indian Creek Trail to the right (northwest), where shrubs and oaks stretch across the meadows. Isolation reaches its peak in this desolate valley; signs of civilization are far removed if you hike on a weekday.

You'll hear the relaxing sounds of Indian Creek, which flows year round. Follow the trail to the soft banks, where overgrown bunchgrass hides the narrow creek. After crossing the water, veer away from Indian Creek Trail and head north (right) along the dirt road. Note: The PCT does not begin until Pioneer Mail Picnic Ground and is only half the hike.

Climbing out of the valley, the trail ascends steeply to the right, slowly levels off after a short distance, and then tunnels beneath a large oak tree that arches over the trail. After traversing grassy plains, the trail crosses Sunrise Highway (County Road S1) and continues at the Pioneer Mail Picnic Ground.

Just past the restrooms at mile 5, pick up the southbound PCT. With the valley to the east, the trail begins to run parallel to Sunrise Highway. The landscape offers views of Cottonwood Canyon below. Multicolored stone protrusions, sun-bleached manzanitas, and wildflowers—like purple lupine and Indian paintbrush—decorate the rim of this narrow slope.

Intersecting the Garnet Peak Trail (see Hike 17), the PCT passes rust-colored boulders, century plants, and towering pines. To the east, the cavernous Storm Canyon opens to a spectacular view, far surpassing that of Cottonwood Canyon. Rather than continuing south (left) on the PCT, head toward the Noble Canyon Trail. This final stretch of the hike traverses forests and chaparral, ending back at the Penny Pines Trail trailhead.

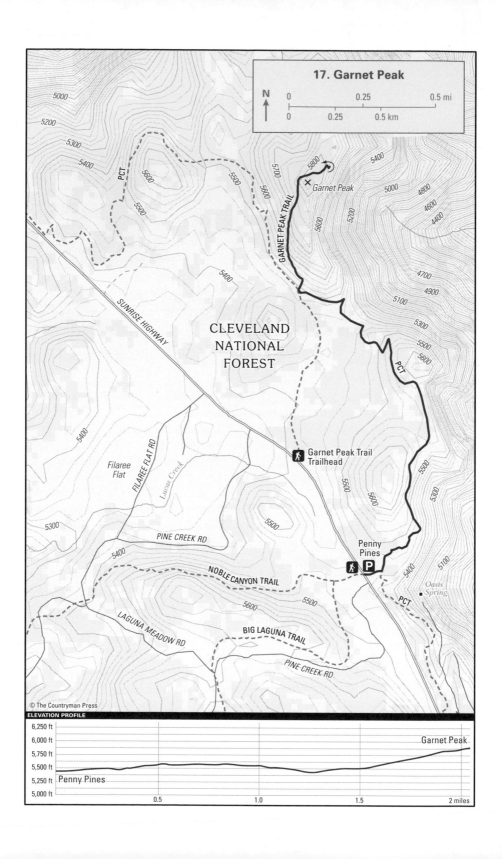

17. Garnet Peak

N

| 0 | | 0.25 | | 0.5 mi |
| 0 | 0.25 | 0.5 km | | |

5000
5200
5300
5400
5600
5500
5500
PCT
5500
5600
5700
5600
5800
5400
5000
4800
4600
4400
Garnet Peak
5600
5200
4700
4900
5100
5300
5500
5600
PCT
SUNRISE HIGHWAY

CLEVELAND
NATIONAL
FOREST

5400

FILAREE FLAT RD
Lucas Creek

Filaree
Flat

PINE CREEK RD

5300
5400
5500
5500

Garnet Peak Trail
Trailhead

5500
5600

Penny
Pines

P

5300
5400
5100

Oasis
Spring

PCT

NOBLE CANYON TRAIL

5600
5500

LAGUNA MEADOW RD

BIG LAGUNA TRAIL

PINE CREEK RD

© The Countryman Press

ELEVATION PROFILE

6,250 ft				
6,000 ft				Garnet Peak
5,750 ft				
5,500 ft				
5,250 ft				
5,000 ft	Penny Pines			
	0.5	1.0	1.5	2 miles

Hike 17

Garnet Peak

Distance: 2.8 miles round-trip

Hiking time: 1.5 hours

Trail highlights: Forest, chaparral fields, panoramic summit view

Difficulty: ▲▲

Family friendly: ▲▲▲

Scenery: ▲▲▲

Solitude: ▲▲

Trail condition: ▲▲

Getting There

Garnet Peak can be accessed from two entry points. Exit Interstate 8 onto Sunrise Highway (County Road S1), and continue north to the trailhead for the Penny Pines Trail at mile marker 27.3. Additional parking is available in the dirt turnout area at mile marker 27.8, where a wooden post marks the Garnet Peak Trail trailhead. Launching from the Penny Pines Trail trailhead, where this hike description begins, will result in a slightly longer hike to the peak. Vehicles must display a National Forest Adventure Pass.

| The route to Garnet Peak Trail

GPS TRAILHEAD COORDINATES

UTM Zone	11S
Easting	550757
Northing	3640921
Latitude	N32.90531°
Longitude	W116.45724°

Overview

Before merging with the Pacific Crest Trail, the Garnet Peak Trail passes through a forest and a chaparral field. The true beauty begins when the trail meets the PCT, which gradually becomes a rock-laden path climbing Garnet Peak.

Considering the brevity of the ascent, the view from the 5,900-foot summit is incredible. On a clear day, hikers can catch a glimpse of Anza-Borrego Desert and the Salton Sea to the east, Monument and Stephenson Peaks to the south, and San Gorgonio to the north. Panoramic views and easy accessibility make Garnet Peak a weekend favorite among hikers.

In Detail

From the Penny Pines Trail trailhead, follow the Big Laguna Trail briefly east as it threads through Jeffrey-pine forest. Baby's breath, wild buckwheat, and lavender-colored chaparral add life to the woodlands. Where towering conifers once stood prior to the 2003 wildfires, scrub oak and chamise now flourish.

Continue along the woodchip trail until it meets the Pacific Crest Trail. Turn left onto the PCT. As you head north, the trail narrows, cutting through a brushy field of Mojave yucca, ceanothus, and stalks of Our Lord's Candle.

After a mile, turn right onto Garnet Peak Trail. For those who started from mile marker 27.8 instead of Penny Pines, you will have crossed the PCT and continued north here.

Changing in terrain, the dirt trail gives way to loose red rock scattered across the path like pebbles in a riverbed. Manzanitas, bleached from the sun, jut out of shrubs lining the trail. During the final ascent, be cautious; many of the rocks are unstable.

| Majestic views of Anza-Borrego Desert, the Laguna Mountains, and Storm Canyon

At the summit, swirled-orange boulders serve as observation decks that overlook the valleys thousands of feet below. Vistas from the jagged crest are truly magnificent, including views of Anza-Borrego Desert, the Laguna Mountains, and Storm Canyon. Rising from the desert floor are mounds, each one skirted by sheets of green. Garnet Peak may offer an ideal photo op, but it tends to be unbearably windy when the Santa Ana winds blow.

To return, head back along the PCT to Penny Pines Trail trailhead, or continue straight along to the trailhead for the Garnet Peak Trail to complete a loop via Sunrise Highway.

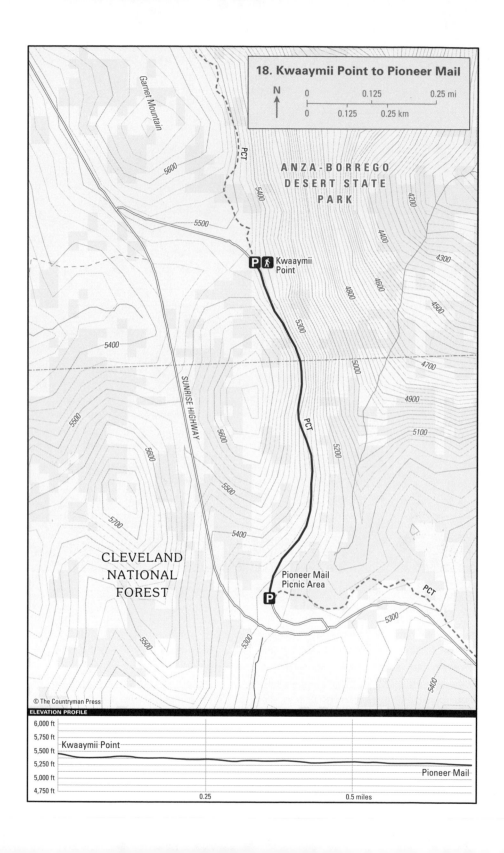

18. Kwaaymii Point to Pioneer Mail

N

| 0 | | 0.125 | | 0.25 mi |
| 0 | 0.125 | | 0.25 km | |

Garnet Mountain

5600

PCT

5400

5500

**A N Z A - B O R R E G O
D E S E R T   S T A T E
P A R K**

4200

4400

4300

4600

4800

P ⚐ Kwaaymii
Point

5300

4500

5400

5000

4700

SUNRISE HIGHWAY

5500

5600

4900

PCT

5100

5600

5400

5700

5200

5500

5400

Pioneer Mail
Picnic Area

PCT

P

5300

CLEVELAND
NATIONAL
FOREST

5500

5300

5300

5400

© The Countryman Press

ELEVATION PROFILE

6,000 ft			
5,750 ft			
5,500 ft	Kwaaymii Point		
5,250 ft			
5,000 ft			Pioneer Mail
4,750 ft			
		0.25	0.5 miles

Hike 18

Kwaaymii Point to Pioneer Mail

Distance: 1 mile round-trip	
Hiking time: 30 minutes	
Trail highlights: Unremitting views, rippled mountains, undemanding trail	
Difficulty: ▲	
Family friendly: ▲▲▲	
Scenery: ▲▲	
Solitude: ▲	
Trail condition: ▲▲▲	

GPS TRAILHEAD COORDINATES

UTM Zone	11S
Easting	548376
Northing	3644134
Latitude	N32.93438°
Longitude	W116.48169°

Getting There

Exit Interstate 8 onto Sunrise Highway (CR S1), and continue north to the paved turnoff at mile marker 30.3. Follow the short road to the circular parking area, which has space for approximately eight cars. The trail can also be accessed via the Pioneer Mail Picnic Ground at mile marker 29.3. The stretch of land between these two parking areas comprises the 30-minute hike. This hike to Kwaaymii Point is not to be confused with the Kwaaymii Nature Trail near the Mount Laguna Visitor Center at mile marker 23.5. A National Forest Adventure Pass is required.

Overview

The brevity of this trip is ideal for hikers of any level wanting a breathtaking view without a lot of work. Note that while the trail is easy and brief, there is a steep drop without a guardrail, so parents must carefully watch their children. Sunrise Highway (County Road S1) provides access to both ends of the trail.

This quick fix of natural beauty peers into Anza-Borrego Desert, bounded by rugged mountains, nearly 4,000 feet below. Deteriorating guardrails and chiseled cliffs show that this path once served as part of the original Sunrise Highway. Although the trail is flat, this elevated stretch is not for those with a fear of heights.

Since this hike is trivially brief, it is best combined with neighboring hikes such as Garnet Peak (Hike 17) or Kwaaymii Point to Sunrise Highway (Hike 19). Otherwise, it is considered more of an "introduction to hiking" for children or an opportunity to access a local viewpoint with minimal effort.

In Detail

This 30-minute hike offers immediate, unbroken views from start to finish. Begin at the Kwaaymii Point parking area, and head south toward the clearly marked Pacific Crest Trail. The orange-dirt trail descends slightly between granite walls on the west and vast desert on the east. Before 1975, this broad path was part of the old Sunrise Highway. Chiseled rock and remnants of retaining walls hint at the road's existence.

You can see the highlight of this brief trek, which follows the rim of Cottonwood Canyon, bounded by the rippled peaks of the Oriflamme Mountains. Patches of vibrant growth bring color to the desert floor, eventually surrendering to an arid landscape that climbs the canyon walls. To the west, towering walls of rust-hued boulders sprout clusters of desert tobacco and chamise. Continue south on the PCT, past manzanitas and wild chaparral, until you reach the Pioneer Mail trailhead at the Pioneer Mail Picnic Area.

Across Sunset Highway, you may still see evidence of the 2003 Cedar Fire, which raged across 262,500 acres of the Cleveland National Forest. In total it destroyed 280,278 acres and killed 15 people until it was contained on November 3. An informational plaque stands directly in front of what was once blackened forest.

Here, at the turnaround point, the Pioneer Mail Picnic Ground makes an ideal spot for lunch. This hike can easily be done in reverse by beginning here rather than at the Kwaaymii Point trailhead.

To extend the return hike, cross the Kwaaymii Point parking area, and head half a mile north on the PCT for even more impressive views. This trail can also be linked to Hikes 17 or 19.

| Devastation from the 2003 Cedar Fire

Hike 19

Kwaaymii Point to Sunrise Highway

Distance: 10 miles round-trip

Hiking time: 4 hours

Trail highlights: Mountain and canyon
views, pink boulders

Difficulty: ▲▲

Family friendly: ▲

Scenery: ▲▲

Solitude: ▲

Trail condition: ▲▲▲

Getting There

Exit Interstate 8 onto Sunrise Highway (CR
S1), and continue north to the paved turnoff
at mile marker 30.3. Follow the short road
to the circular Kwaaymii Point parking area,
which has space for approximately eight
cars. You can extend the hike by one mile by
starting from the Pioneer Mail Picnic Area,
just south, at mile marker 29.3. The shaded
area of Pioneer Mail has picnic tables, restrooms, and water. Vehicles must display a
National Forest Adventure Pass.

GPS TRAILHEAD COORDINATES

UTM Zone	11S
Easting	548376
Northing	3644134
Latitude	N32.93438°
Longitude	W116.48169°

Overview

From Cottonwood Canyon to the Oriflamme
Mountains, the unremitting views of this
10-mile hike make it worthwhile. Along the
rim of the canyon, the trail begins just beyond the destruction from the 2002 Pines
Fire, which started after a National Guard
helicopter hit a power line. The region also
suffered damage from the 2003 Cedar Fire,
which was started by a lost hunter and vio-
lently driven by Santa Ana winds.

The northward climb out of the Laguna
Mountains enters Cuyamaca Rancho State
Park, which covers more than 26,000 acres
of oak and pine forest. Switchbacks give
way to fantastic rock formations and irides-
cent Canterbury bells, overshadowed only
by the Oriflamme Canyon in the distance.
Although this hike parallels Sunrise Highway
(County Road S1), traffic can be heard only
at the beginning and end.

In Detail

From the Kwaaymii Point parking area, head
north on the Pacific Crest Trail. Departing the
Laguna Mountains, the PCT cuts through
scrub oak and manzanitas. A quarter mile
into the hike, the chaparral slopes give way
to jagged pink boulders that dominate the
remainder of the journey.

Hugging the east shoulder of Cottonwood Canyon, the narrow trail offers sprawl-
ing views of the Anza-Borrego Desert. In the
springtime, Canadian thistle, prickly phlox,

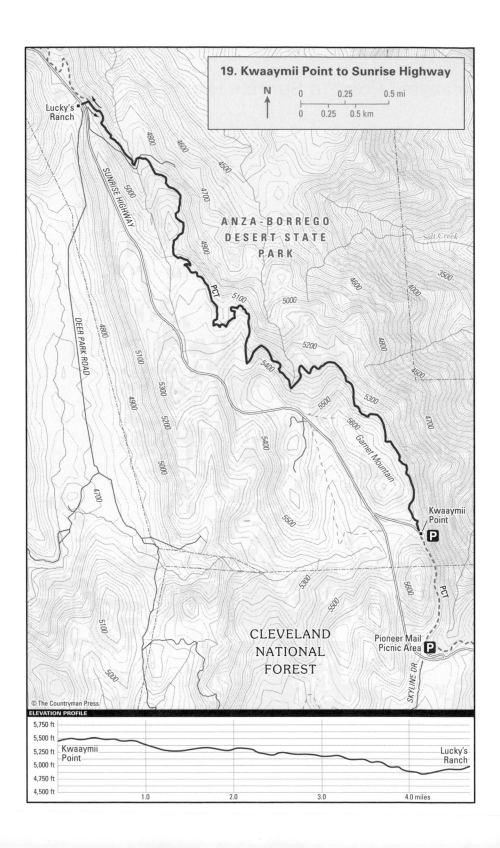

19. Kwaaymii Point to Sunrise Highway

N

| 0 | | 0.25 | | 0.5 mi |
| 0 | 0.25 | 0.5 km | | |

Lucky's
Ranch

4800
4600
4500
5000
4700
SUNRISE HIGHWAY
4900
PCT
5100
5000
5200

ANZA-BORREGO
DESERT STATE
PARK

Salt Creek

3500
4600
4800
4000
4500
4700

DEER PARK ROAD
4800
5100
5300
4900
5200
5000
5400
5400
5300
5500
5600
Garnet Mountain

Kwaaymii
Point

P

5600

4700

5300
5500
5100

CLEVELAND
NATIONAL
FOREST

Pioneer Mail
Picnic Area

P

PCT

SKYLINE DR

5000

© The Countryman Press

ELEVATION PROFILE

5,750 ft				
5,500 ft				
5,250 ft	Kwaaymii			Lucky's
5,000 ft	Point			Ranch
4,750 ft				
4,500 ft	1.0	2.0	3.0	4.0 miles

| Leaving the Laguna Mountains

Canterbury bells, and evening primrose dot the rock canyon walls.

After a gradual ascent, the trail enters an area heavily populated with manzanitas, many of which appear fossilized from the bleaching of the sun. You can see the occasional jackrabbit or grouse hiding out in this area. Be wary of the nightshade flowers, which bloom during April and May. These lavender blossoms produce tomato-like berries that are extremely poisonous.

Spring hikers will notice scarlet buglers growing along the trailside. Here the trail ascends northwest, away from the canyon, before switching back northeast at about the 2-mile point. A gradual climb on the rocky trail leads to breathtaking views of Oriflamme Mountain. Framing the trail are mounds of red rock formations that fit together like gigantic puzzle pieces.

Upon crossing a sandy wash, the trail traverses boulder slabs next to a deep ravine. A series of switchbacks leads to an intersecting jeep road after 4 miles. Continue

on the PCT, which drops slightly west into a chaparral valley before heading directly north, ever closer to Sunrise Highway. Lining the path in this final stretch are woolly blue curls, famous for their leaves, which are purported to cure ulcers and alleviate pain.

The east view opens onto Oriflamme Canyon, with Oriflamme Mountain as the backdrop. The name *Oriflamme*, meaning "golden flame," is derived from the sparks of static electricity that are sometimes seen when desert sands blow against the quartz mountain. Just before reaching 5 miles, turn left onto the narrow spur trail that heads west toward Sunrise Highway.

The turnaround point is across from Lucky's Ranch at the 33-mile marker on Sunrise Highway. To cut the distance in half, shuttle back to the Kwaaymii Point parking area via Sunrise Highway. Otherwise, hike south on the PCT in the direction from which you came. On the return half of this hike, the southbound view offers vistas that may have been overlooked during the northbound leg.

| Agua Caliente Creek |

PART II

Cuyamaca Rancho State Park, Anza-Borrego Desert, and San Felipe Wilderness Area

| Century plant in Anza-Borrego Desert |

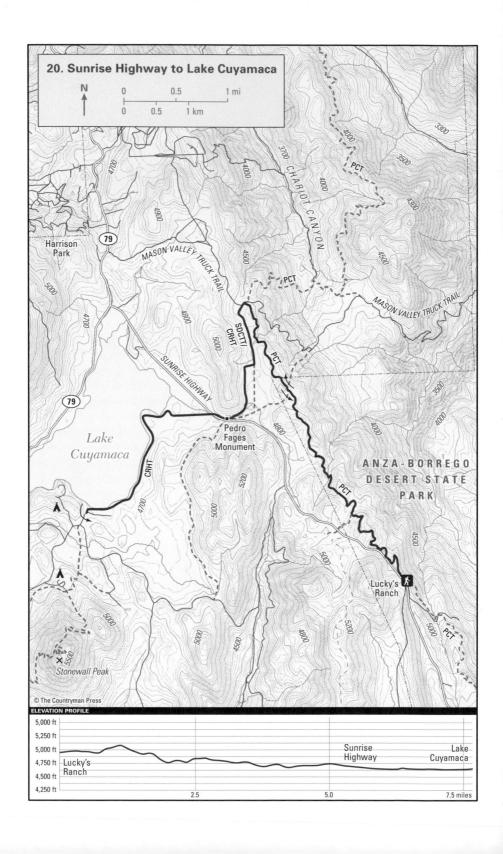

20. Sunrise Highway to Lake Cuyamaca

N

| 0 | 0.5 | 1 mi |
| 0 | 0.5 | 1 km |

Harrison Park

79

Lake Cuyamaca

79

MASON VALLEY TRUCK TRAIL

SDCTT CRHT

SUNRISE HIGHWAY

CRHT

Pedro Fages Monument

CHARIOT CANYON

PCT

PCT

PCT

MASON VALLEY TRUCK TRAIL

ANZA-BORREGO DESERT STATE PARK

PCT

Lucky's Ranch

PCT

Stonewall Peak

© The Countryman Press

ELEVATION PROFILE

5,000 ft				
5,250 ft				
5,000 ft			Sunrise Highway	Lake Cuyamaca
4,750 ft	Lucky's Ranch			
4,500 ft				
4,250 ft		2.5	5.0	7.5 miles

Hike 20

Sunrise Highway to Lake Cuyamaca

Distance: 15 miles round-trip

Hiking time: 9 hours

Trail highlights: Canyon and lake views, pleasant meadows

Difficulty: ▲▲

Family friendly: ▲

Scenery: ▲▲

Solitude: ▲▲

Trail condition: ▲▲▲

Getting There

Exit Interstate 8 onto Sunrise Highway (CR S1), and continue north to the paved turnoff across from Lucky 5 Ranch at mile marker 33. Parking is free in "turn-out" sites where not prohibited. The trail drops down from Sunrise Highway on the east side of the road and joins the PCT less than 100 feet into the hike.

GPS TRAILHEAD COORDINATES

UTM Zone	11S
Easting	545431
Northing	3648158
Latitude	N32.97083°
Longitude	W116.51383°

Overview

Dropping down from Sunrise Highway (County Road S1), this 15-mile hike seems to improve with every step. It is, however, void of shade during most of this stretch of the PCT, so plan accordingly. The trail offers sweeping views of Oriflamme Canyon to the east, fronted with subtle surprises of mariposa lily blossoms. The smell of sage, the vibrant colors of spring wildflowers, and the post-fire landscape make this hike enjoyable. Chaparral slopes and manzanita trees fade as the trail splits away from the PCT and enters a meadow of chamise. Here, wild oaks provide the first hint of shade, giving way to fields of snapdragons and blazing stars. After crossing Sunrise Highway, the landscape appears more colorful, with a green meadow framing Lake Cuyamaca in the distance.

In Detail

Begin on the narrow dirt path just below Sunrise Highway. When this path intersects the PCT, head north (left) so that the canyon view is to your right. Slowly pushing away from the paralleling highway, the PCT runs through chaparral slopes of chamise, Our Lord's Candle, and beavertail cactus. The scent of sage fills the air during a brief northeast climb.

Cross over a ravine before entering the steepest section of the hike. Fortunately, this brief climb levels out on the shrub-filled

| Lake Cuyamaca

slopes that overlook Oriflamme Canyon. Continue north, switching back several times before approaching a spur trail leading back to Sunrise Highway (where water is available, 0.25 miles from the PCT.)

Pass the spur trail and continue on the PCT. Cross another dip and ascend past rust-colored slabs. These weathered rocks break in parallel planes, often revealing swirled patterns of red and black. The trail sinks past manzanita trees and chamise. In springtime, pink Canadian thistles sprout from the path's shoulder. The terrain changes from desert to meadows.

A gradual climb before the 3-mile point leads to an open slope that overlooks cleared flatlands to the west. In the distance is the first sign of Lake Cuyamaca. Continue

northwest on the PCT; you may see quail. The trail parallels a meadow where manzanitas jut from the earth.

Just after 4 miles, leave the PCT and head west (left) down the old jeep road. A metal gate marks the entrance to the California Riding and Hiking Trail. Just past the gate, take the left fork onto the San Diego Trans County Trail, which originates in Del Mar. You will have descended more than 300 feet in elevation since the trailhead.

The oaks scattered throughout this meadow offer welcoming shade. Pass through a second gate, and continue along the gravel road. Canterbury bells and western wallflowers splatter the fields with color during May and June. Just before the 5-mile point, veer right onto the California Rid-

| Views of Oriflamme Mountain

ing and Hiking Trail rather than continuing straight on the jeep trail. At the time of writing, this brief detour was intended for the purpose of vegetation re-growth. Now approaching a large oak, you will have entered the heart of a pleasant meadow. Clusters of lavender snapdragons decorate the field, their tranquil beauty contrasting with the sounds of Sunrise Highway traffic. Continue southwest through a metal gate that opens onto Sunrise Highway at milepost 36.

You can either turn back here or continue to Lake Cuyamaca. To reach the water, cross the highway and stay on the California Riding and Hiking Trail, heading west. The trail passes through a grassy plain of oaks and purple lupines.

You get a clear view of the lake and the surrounding fields at 6 miles. The path begins to skirt away from the water, so leave the trail at 6.5 miles, and cut directly over the slopes toward the lake. To complete this there-and-back hike, return the way you came. However, if you wish to spend the night, camping is available on the shores of Lake Cuyamaca in the town of Julian (15027 Highway 79). The park is closed December through March.

Tent sites are available on a reserved basis. Campfires and swimming are not permitted. Be aware that this family-friendly campground can be crowded due to trout fishing and duck hunting in season. For more information, call 760-765-0515. A tackle shop, convenience store, and restaurant are just beyond the campground.

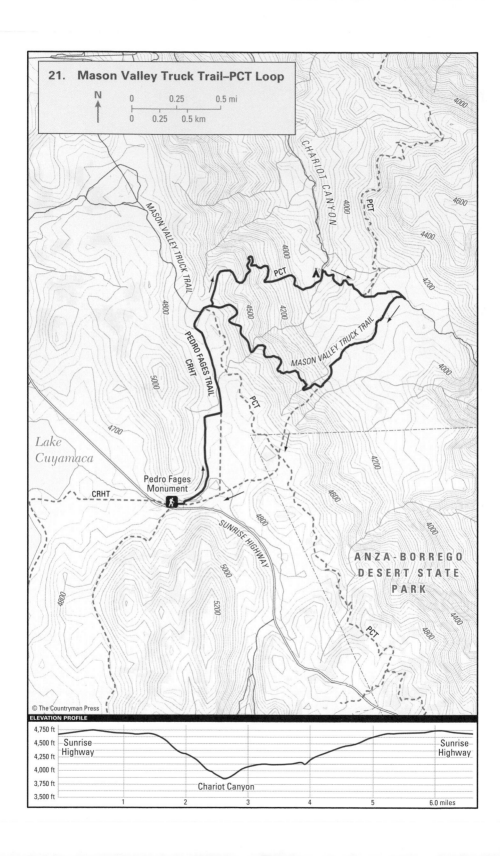

21. Mason Valley Truck Trail–PCT Loop

N

| 0 | 0.25 | 0.5 mi |
| 0 | 0.25 | 0.5 km |

CHARIOT CANYON

PCT

MASON VALLEY TRUCK TRAIL

PCT

PCT

MASON VALLEY TRUCK TRAIL

PEDRO FAGES TRAIL

CRHT

PCT

Lake Cuyamaca

Pedro Fages Monument

CRHT

SUNRISE HIGHWAY

ANZA-BORREGO DESERT STATE PARK

PCT

© The Countryman Press

ELEVATION PROFILE

4,750 ft						
4,500 ft	Sunrise Highway					Sunrise Highway
4,250 ft						
4,000 ft						
3,750 ft			Chariot Canyon			
3,500 ft						
	1	2	3	4	5	6.0 miles

Hike 21
Mason Valley Truck Trail–PCT Loop

Distance: 6.5-mile loop

Hiking time: 4 hours

Trail highlights: Meadow, canyon views, creek crossing, rewarding ascent

Difficulty: ▲▲▲

Family friendly: ▲

Scenery: ▲▲▲

Solitude: ▲▲▲

Trail condition: ▲▲▲

Getting There

Exit Interstate 8 onto Sunrise Highway (CR S1), and continue north to the turnoff at mile marker 36. The trail can also be accessed by taking Interstate 8 east to Highway 79 north until you see Lake Cuyamaca. The trailhead is 1.7 miles east of Highway 79, approximately 8 miles from the quaint town of Julian. No permits are required for parking in turn-out sites. The trail starts at the east side of Sunrise Highway just beyond the Pedro Fages Monument.

GPS TRAILHEAD COORDINATES

UTM Zone	11S
Easting	542723
Northing	3650734
Latitude	N32.99418°
Longitude	W116.54269°

Overview

The initial stroll along Pedro Fages Trail sets the tone for this picturesque journey. After cutting through a meadow, the route briefly joins the Mason Valley Truck Trail, offering views of Chariot Mountain to the north. To form the second half of the loop, the wide dirt road connects with the Pacific Coast Trail, which features chaparral slopes and California poppies in spring. During a canyon ascent, gray boulders and yellow brittle-brush give way to red rocks and bouquets of white yarrow. The challenging climb out of Chariot Canyon is as rewarding as it is demanding. Hikers can find shade under the oaks just beyond the ridge. Leveling out, the final stretch traverses the same grassy fields of Canterbury bells and western wallflowers crossed at the outset, providing a tranquil cool down.

In Detail

The trip begins on the Pedro Fages Trail, named for Colonel Pedro Fages, who arrived in San Diego Bay in 1769. The Catalan soldier led the shipborne segment of the Gaspar de Portolá expedition that explored much of Southern and Central California. He was appointed governor of the Californias in 1782.

From the Pedro Fages Monument, head into a meadow predominated by snapdragons and Canterbury bells in spring. If the road is blocked to allow for plant growth, follow the trail to the left of the meadow, past a large oak. Linking back with the road, the trail passes manzanitas skirted by brittlebrushes and mariposa lilies.

After passing through a small metal gate, turn right at the trail intersection and pass through much larger metal gate leading to Mason Valley Truck Trail. Just beyond the gate and below a concrete box, an emergency water spigot used by firefighters is available.

Now on the Mason Valley Truck Trail, cross over the southbound PCT, which spills from Oriflamme Canyon into Chariot Canyon. Briefly continue on the Mason Valley Truck Trail, now linked with northbound PCT, past chaparral slopes of sage and yarrow. The truck trail will split off to your right, but continue on the northbound PCT.

Nearly 2 miles into the trip, the trail crosses a stone bridge over a deep ravine.

Views of Oriflamme Canyon slowly fade into the purple-hued magnificence of Chariot Mountain.

Now forming the northern portion of the loop, the PCT is landscaped with massive gray boulders and towering stalks of Our Lord's Candle. The descent into the canyon offers an excellent vantage point for viewing the already-traversed portion of the trail. Just before dipping into a wash, the PCT branches north, to the left. Leave the PCT and continue straight.

Bring enough water for this steep ascent out of the canyon that continues just over 1 mile. Here the terrain alternates between fine sand and rugged rock, visited only by the occasional hummingbird, rabbit, and lizard. Head right onto the Mason Valley Truck Trail, and continue to close the loop of the hike. Eventually it will intersect with the PCT. Leave the Mason Valley Truck Trail, and head back toward the trailhead where the

| White prickly poppy

| Mason Valley Truck Trail

journey began. The final 1.4 miles follows the original route, past the metal gate, onto Pedro Fages Trail and into the meadow that meets Sunrise Highway (County Road S1).

If time permits, cross Sunrise Highway, and continue 1.5 miles west on the San Diego Trans County Trail to Lake Cuyamaca. (The name means "the place where it rains.") From May through September, Cuyamaca Rancho State Park offers several exhibits, including the Stonewall Mine, which chronicles the history of gold mining in Southern California. For exhibits on local plants and animals, stop by the Interpretive Center at Paso Picacho on Highway 79. There is also a cultural museum at the park's headquarters. The park itself is home to ponderosa, Coulter, and Jeffrey pines, live oaks, and a variety of wildlife, including badgers, foxes, mountain lions, and bobcats.

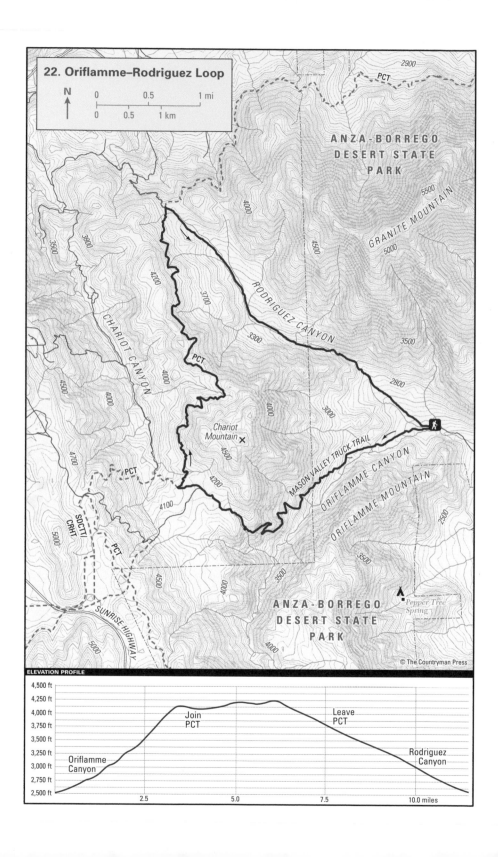

22. Oriflamme–Rodriguez Loop

N
0   0.5   1 mi
0   0.5   1 km

PCT   2900

ANZA-BORREGO
DESERT STATE
PARK

4000   5500

4500   GRANITE MOUNTAIN   5000

3500
3800
4200   RODRIGUEZ CANYON
3700   3300   3500

CHARIOT CANYON

4000   PCT   2800

4700   4000   3000

4100   Chariot
        Mountain ×   4500
                        4200   MASON VALLEY TRUCK TRAIL

PCT   4000   ORIFLAMME CANYON

SDCTI
CRHT   PCT   ORIFLAMME MOUNTAIN   2900

5000   4100

                        4500   3500

SUNRISE HIGHWAY   4000

5000   ANZA-BORREGO
                                            DESERT STATE   Pepper Tree
                                            PARK   Spring

                        4000

© The Countryman Press

ELEVATION PROFILE

4,500 ft
4,250 ft
4,000 ft   Join   Leave
3,750 ft   PCT   PCT
3,500 ft
3,250 ft
3,000 ft   Oriflamme   Rodriguez
2,750 ft   Canyon   Canyon
2,500 ft
            2.5   5.0   7.5   10.0 miles

Hike 22

Oriflamme–Rodriguez Loop

Getting There

From CA 78 east, turn right onto County Road S2, also known as Southern Overland Stage Road. Just after Box Canyon historical site, turn west at mile 26.8, onto Mason Valley Truck Trail until it meets the Rodriguez Spur Truck Trail. Veer right at the fork marked "Oriflamme Canyon." At the end of this 3-mile bumpy road is a dirt lot where the Rodriguez Canyon Road begins. Because of soft sand and jutting rocks, only four-wheel vehicles can reach this trailhead.

GPS TRAILHEAD COORDINATES	
UTM Zone	11S
Easting	548571
Northing	3653464
Latitude	N33.01855°
Longitude	W116.47995°

Overview

Near Box Canyon, site of a historic early wagon road, is Mason Valley Truck Trail, the first leg of this three-section hike. Climbing into the vastness of Oriflamme Canyon, this rutted road was once a Native American pathway. The U.S. Post Office used it to transport mail via horseback and mule from San Antonio to San Diego in 1857. Nearly 75 years later, a more substantial Mason Valley Truck Trail was built. The rutted road, now closed to vehicles, provides a wide, safe hiking link between County Roads S2 and S1.

On this hike, after the initial monotony of the truck trail, you switch to the pleasant Pacific Crest Trail, which feeds in from the north. This journey is most enjoyable in the springtime, when slopes come alive with buttercups, poppies, and Indian paintbrush. Eventually the narrow trail intersects with Rodriguez Canyon Road, which descends 4 miles east to complete the loop.

In Detail

Although you can hike this loop in either direction, it's better to begin on the Mason Valley Truck Trail, which forks left from the trailhead through Oriflamme Canyon. Going in that direction will send you past a stream and through shaded campsites, making the demanding ascent more bearable.

| Our Lord's Candle sprouting pink blossoms

Within the first few steps, signs of a desert landscape are made apparent by the teddy bear and beavertail cacti that sprout magenta and yellow blossoms from their thorned pads in season. Just short of 1 mile, a spur trail heads left to the creek bank while the Mason Valley Truck Trail continues straight. For an overnight hike, take the 2.6-mile (one-way) left-hand spur to reach Pepper Tree Spring. This area offers cascading waterfalls, shallow pools, trickling streams, and sycamore-shaded campsites.

For a day hike, keep going straight on the Mason Valley Truck Trail, which runs

Just past this point, the trail enters a plain of prickly poppies, Indian paintbrush, and buttercups blooming in season. Pass the spur trails to the left and continue until the PCT appears to your right, around 4 miles.

Beginning the second (and most pleasant) leg of the hike, head north on the PCT into a valley of bush poppies, purple lupines, and goldfields. Providing refreshing changes in terrain, the narrow trail winds, climbs, and dips through Chariot Canyon.

In May and June, hillsides resemble a Dr. Seuss scene, as hundreds of Our Lord's Candles sprout pink blossoms. Sandwiched between Chariot Canyon to the west and Chariot Mountain to the east, this section of the PCT also offers views of Granite Mountain as it meets Rodriguez Canyon Road.

Leave the PCT and head east (right) on Rodriguez Canyon Road, a wide jeep road similar in appearance to the Mason Valley Truck Trail. During the 4-mile descent, the road bends southeast to skirt Granite Mountain. Signaling the end of the long journey is sight of the Mason Valley Truck Trail, which parallels Rodriguez Canyon Road toward the end of the hike, all the way back to the parking area.

alongside a gurgling stream. In spring, goldfields and daisy-like brittlebrush dot the arid slopes. As the trail leaves the stream, the most grueling portion of the hike begins. Devoid of shade or lush terrain, the climb along Oriflamme Canyon has a few switchbacks before leveling off at a 4,130-foot peak.

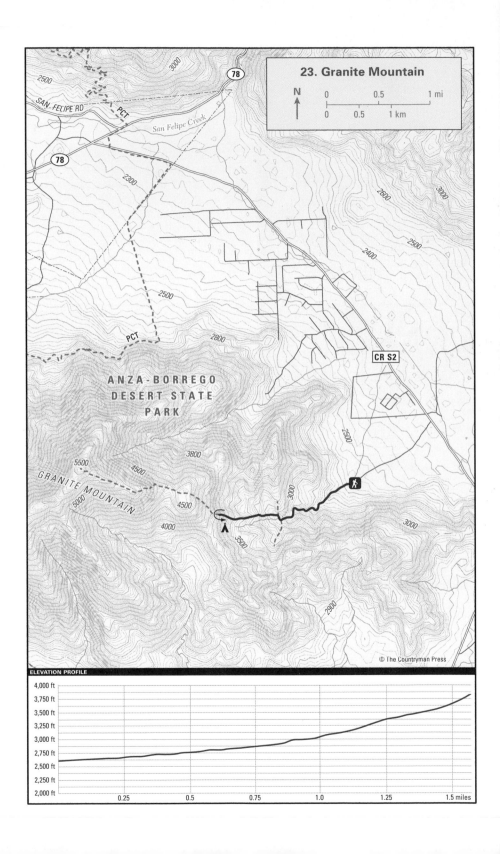

23. Granite Mountain

N

| 0 | | 0.5 | | 1 mi |

| 0 | 0.5 | 1 km |

78

San Felipe Creek

SAN FELIPE RD

PCT

78

2500

3000

2300

2500

PCT

2800

2600

3000

2400

2500

CR S2

A N Z A - B O R R E G O
D E S E R T   S T A T E
P A R K

2500

3800

5500

4500

G R A N I T E   M O U N T A I N

5000

4500

4000

3000

3500

3000

2900

© The Countryman Press

ELEVATION PROFILE

| | 0.25 | 0.5 | 0.75 | 1.0 | 1.25 | 1.5 miles |

4,000 ft
3,750 ft
3,500 ft
3,250 ft
3,000 ft
2,750 ft
2,500 ft
2,250 ft
2,000 ft

Hike 23

Granite Mountain

Distance: 3 miles round-trip

Hiking time: 1.5 hours

Trail highlights: Desert flowers, boulder
 ascent, mountain views

Difficulty: ▲ ▲ ▲ ▲

Family friendly: Not recommended

Scenery: ▲ ▲

Solitude: ▲ ▲ ▲

Trail condition: ▲

Getting There

Head east on CA 78 through Julian, a quaint
town famous for its pies. Eleven miles past
Julian, turn right onto County Road S2
(Great Southern Overland Stage Road),
which cuts through Anza-Borrego Desert.
At the 21.5-mile marker, turn right and follow
the bumpy dirt road 1 mile west until it ends
at the trailhead. Finding a parking space will
not be a problem; few attempt this hike because of its arid terrain and lack of shade. A
parking permit is not required.

GPS TRAILHEAD COORDINATES

UTM Zone	11S
Easting	552774
Northing	3656690
Latitude	N33.04745°
Longitude	W116.43477°

Overview

This challenging trail climbs the shoulder of
Granite Mountain, located in the southwest
corner of Anza-Borrego Desert State Park.
Although there is no access trail between
the PCT and the summit, you can hike the
mountain from several directions and enjoy
views of the Salton Sea. Less than 1 mile
into the trek, the hiker will have faced such
challenges as steep boulder climbs, thick
brush, and lack of shade. The adventurous
hiker can continue past a primitive campsite
at a 4,624-foot peak to enjoy breathtaking
views from Granite Mountain's summit at
5,633 feet.

Although this hike is short, it can be
lengthened all the way to the summit, extend-
ing the distance to 6.5 miles round-trip. Keep
in mind that the dry, hot environment makes
it demanding. The terrain shifts dramatically
from low- to high-desert landscapes from the
trail's starting point at Blair Valley. Dwarfed
by eight-foot agave plants, brightly colored
brittlebrush flowers sprout from the rocks.
After meandering a boulder trail, the path
narrows and gradually ascends past clusters of Mojave yucca, white sage, and cholla
cactus. During the spring, cactus flowers
pleasantly splash the arid terrain, showing
off their bright shades of fuchsia and lime.
The surreal shapes of the metamorphic rock,
however, make this trail special.

Legend has it that "spirit flames" are vis-

| Cactus flowers

ible on Oriflamme Mountain, just south of Granite Mountain. Since the 1880s, people have mined the east side of the mountain, hoping the magical glimmers signified the presence of gold. Scientists have since concluded that the "flames" are actually static electricity caused by desert winds blowing coarse sand against the quartz boulders.

In Detail

To catch a glimpse of Granite Mountain, begin at the end of the 1-mile-long dirt road off County Road S2. During April and May, keep your windows rolled up: Hundreds of crickets swarm this dusty stretch.

From the trailhead, hike the center trail west through the dry valley. Closed in by walls of granite and metamorphic rock, the 8-foot-wide path begins to narrow and gradually ascend. Amid cholla cactus and Mojave yucca are bushels of yellow brittlebrush, white onion, and blue-eyed grass. Hot pink hedgehog and beavertail cactus flowers bloom among the thorns.

The first major climb begins at 0.3 miles, where large boulders obstruct the path. At the base of the rocks, the spicy scent of white sage perfumes the air. In spring, mon-

arch butterflies dance around milkweeds while lizards scramble up sun-warmed granite slabs. From the base of the valley to the tops of the brushy slopes are patches of purple monkshood, baby blue eyes, and peach-colored desert globe mallow.

Just before the 1-mile mark, scale a series of large boulders, where the trail forks in two directions. The left trail leads to Rodriguez Canyon, while the right trail leads northwest to Granite Mountain. Take the right fork, and continue 100 feet past the split until the trail divides again. This time, head left for a steeper ascent toward the summit. Avoid the trail to the far right as it will narrow and eventually come to a dead end. As you continue, the landscape transitions from sparse patches of dandelions and goldfields to thick, thorny shrubs that envelop the trail.

At 1 mile, a massive, three-tiered rock slab crosses the trail. This steep climb over glossy boulders should not be attempted alone. From this point onward, plan to scale a series of rocks and scramble past thick brush.

After taking in the view of the North Pinyon Mountains to the east, hikers can either retrace their steps to the trailhead or continue 2.15 miles one-way (past a flat campsite) toward Granite Mountain's peak. Keep in mind that there is no defined trail leading all the way to the summit. Those who make it as far as the saddle will see the distant PCT meandering around Granite's northern flank. Beyond that point, the trail fades into deer and mountain lion tracks, overgrown with shrubs. The rewards of this ascent are panoramic views of the San Gabriel Mountains, San Jacinto Peak, and the Salton Sea.

For those who wish to camp in this area, there are developed sites in Anza-Borrego at Tamarisk Grove, Vern Whitaker, and Borrego Palm Canyon. For fees and reservations, call 800-444-7275.

| The route to Granite Mountain

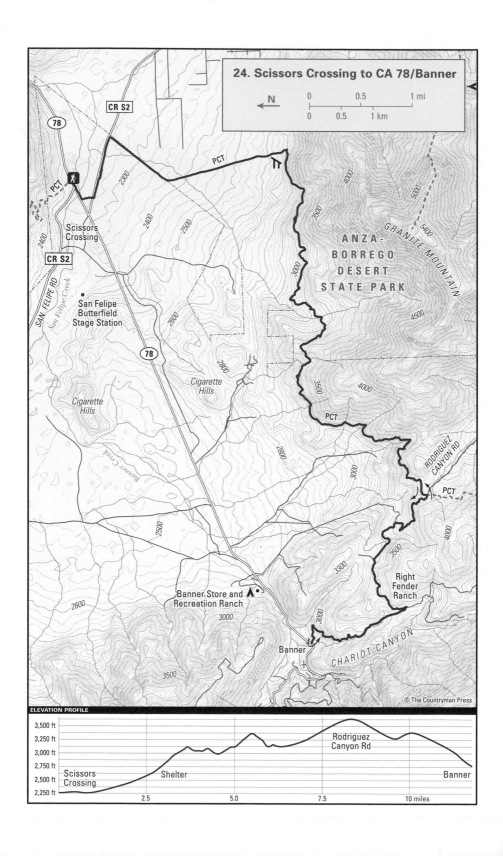

24. Scissors Crossing to CA 78/Banner

N

| 0 | 0.5 | 1 mi |
| 0 | 0.5 | 1 km |

CR S2

78

PCT

PCT

Scissors
Crossing

CR S2

SAN FELIPE RD

San Felipe Creek

San Felipe
Butterfield
Stage Station

78

Cigarette
Hills

Cigarette
Hills

Banner Creek

ANZA-
BORREGO
DESERT
STATE PARK

GRANITE MOUNTAIN

PCT

RODRIGUEZ CANYON RD

PCT

Right
Fender
Ranch

Banner Store and
Recreatiion Ranch

Banner

CHARIOT CANYON

© The Countryman Press

ELEVATION PROFILE

3,500 ft
3,250 ft
3,000 ft
2,750 ft
2,500 ft
2,250 ft

Scissors
Crossing

Shelter

Rodriguez
Canyon Rd

Banner

2.5   5.0   7.5   10 miles

Hike 24

Scissors Crossing to CA 78/Banner

Distance: 24 miles round-trip or 12 miles
with shuttle

Hiking time: 12 hours

Trail highlights: Breathtaking panoramas,
picturesque farms, abandoned gold
mines, mountain-skirting trail

Difficulty: ▲▲▲▲

Family friendly: Not recommended

Scenery: ▲▲

Solitude: ▲▲▲

Trail condition: ▲▲▲

Getting There

From Interstate 15, take CA 78 east for approximately 51 miles. The PCT trailhead at Scissors Crossing is on CA 78 near the intersection of CR S2. Ample parking is available at the intersection. Parking permits are not required.

GPS TRAILHEAD COORDINATES

UTM Zone	11S
Easting	549374
Northing	3662362
Latitude	N33.09878°
Longitude	W116.47088°

Overview

This lengthy hike can best be enjoyed by starting at Scissors Crossing and shuttling back to the trailhead after reaching the mid-

way point at CA 78. Otherwise, hikers can overnight at Banner Recreation Ranch before hiking back the following day.

Either way, most of this hike is spent on the Pacific Crest Trail, skirting the 5,633-foot Granite Mountain. Although the PCT never quite reaches the peak, the gradual ascent along the ridge climbs high enough to offer impressive views of the North Pinyon and Grapevine Mountains. This trail compensates for its lack of water and shade by showcasing the beauty of San Felipe Valley. Nestled in the pastures at its base are several farms and burrowed gold mines. Just before breaking away from the PCT, hikers pass a concrete trough where they can cool off with flowing water. The 3.3-mile stretch to CA 78 follows a jeep road, gently descending through Chariot Canyon.

In Detail

Enter the PCT on the south side of CA 78 at Scissors Crossing, where 78 intersects County Road S2, also known as Great Southern Overland Stage Road. From 1857 until 1861, the Butterfield Stage Line used this route, now a two-lane highway, to transport mail.

The trail begins by paralleling CA 78 and crossing San Felipe Creek. After passing a nature trail to the left, you'll enter a cattle gate that opens onto a field of overgrown shrubs. A birding trail branches off just before the PCT crosses CR S2.

A second metal gate marks the entrance

| View of the Volcan Mountains

to an arid trek toward the base of Granite Mountain. Follow the faint trail that bends left past a water cache graciously provided by the "PCT Trail Ratz," Dave, Dave, and John. Commonly referred to as "Trail Angels" there are dozens of these kindhearted individuals that offer free water and supply stations to hikers along the PCT.

At the time of writing, sections of the trail were overgrown with catclaw shrubs, that can leave hikers snagged and scratched. After briefly dropping and leveling out, the trail breaks south, leaving CR S2 behind. Punctuating the desert are teddy bear and beavertail cacti, century plants, and Mojave yuccas. Jackrabbits and horned lizards seem almost tame in this area, casually staring at passing hikers. The terrain alternates between sand and red rock, and the path

slightly inclines toward Granite Mountain straight ahead. Bits of crystal quartz, scattered below the bark-shedding branches of elephant trees, sparkle in the desert sun.

Cross a fire swath and head through Earthquake Valley. You'll ascend slightly before heading southwest along the PCT, which begins to skirt the base of Granite Mountain.

A boulder overhang just before 3 miles provides the area's only shade. This breezy refuge is the ideal spot to catch your breath and admire the northwest view of the Volcan Mountains. Just before 4 miles, switchbacks begin relentlessly climbing, finally ending at a rocky knoll. There, you'll begin a slight descent toward a small ranch, the trail dropping yet farther before ascending westward. The route briefly detours onto public lands because of landowners who wouldn't let the PCT cross their property. Here you can see the entrance to an abandoned gold mine dating back to 1869.

Thick chaparral slopes set the backdrop as the trail gains elevation across the shoulder of the mountain. Clusters of brittlebrush and sage line the trail, adding life and color to this otherwise bland section. Just beyond 7 miles, the trail dips into a wash before heading south, farther onto flanks of Granite Mountain.

Bushels of catclaws, their thorny branches cradling fuzzy, pale flowers, frame a series of massive gray boulders. The trail cuts through a slope of popcorn flowers and rabbitbrush, prominent in spring. Approaching a jeep road, the landscape changes slightly, offering manzanitas and chamises. After passing under power lines, the route intersects with Rodriguez Truck Trail, where unpurified water is available behind a cleared patch of grass.

This junction marks the meeting of Banner Canyon to the north and Chariot Canyon to the south. Leave the PCT and head northwest (right) along Rodriguez Canyon access road, which provides beautiful views of San Felipe Valley. (Thru-hikers can continue southbound on the PCT rather than turning northwest toward Banner.)

Pass through a barbed-wire gate, and follow the road to the left. Just beyond Right Fender Ranch, fork to the right at 10.6 miles. Crawl under a locked cattle guard to descend north toward your destination of CA 78.

The shade of an old oak and cold drinks at the nearby Banner Store offer the perfect welcome after the long and tiring journey. Half a mile east (right) is Banner Recreation Ranch (36342 Highway 78), where overnight camping is available at 50 campsites. Services include restrooms, showers, drinking water, and an onsite store. The campground, open from May through September, does not require reservations. For more information, contact 760-765-0813.

From CA 78, hikers can either reverse course by hiking 12 miles back to Scissors Crossing or shuttle by car to the trailhead by way of CA 78.

| Jackrabbit near Granite Mountain

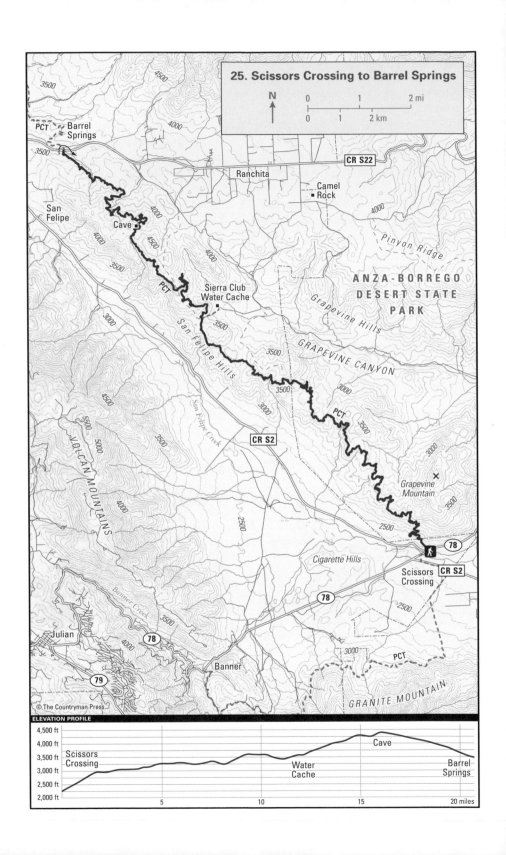

25. Scissors Crossing to Barrel Springs

N

| 0 | | 1 | | 2 mi |
| 0 | 1 | | 2 km | |

PCT
Barrel Springs

CR S22

Ranchita

Camel Rock

San Felipe

Cave

PCT

Sierra Club Water Cache

San Felipe Hills

San Felipe Creek

CR S2

VOLCAN MOUNTAINS

ANZA-BORREGO DESERT STATE PARK

Pinyon Ridge

Grapevine Hills

GRAPEVINE CANYON

PCT

Grapevine Mountain ×

Cigarette Hills

78

Scissors Crossing

CR S2

78

2500

3000

PCT

Banner Creek

Julian

78

Banner

79

GRANITE MOUNTAIN

© The Countryman Press

ELEVATION PROFILE

Scissors Crossing

Water Cache

Cave

Barrel Springs

4,500 ft
4,000 ft
3,500 ft
3,000 ft
2,500 ft
2,000 ft

5   10   15   20 miles

Hike 25

Scissors Crossing to Barrel Springs

Distance: 46 miles round-trip or 23 with shuttle	
Hiking time: 18 hours	
Trail highlights: Towering agave, ocotillo clusters, mountain vistas	
Difficulty: ▲▲▲▲	
Family friendly: Not recommended	
Scenery: ▲▲	
Solitude: ▲▲	
Trail condition: ▲▲▲	

GPS TRAILHEAD COORDINATES

UTM Zone	11S
Easting	549374
Northing	3662362
Latitude	N33.09878°
Longitude	W116.47088°

Getting There

From Interstate 15, take CA 78 east for approximately 51 miles. If time permits, stop in the quaint town of Julian at the intersection of CA 78 and CA 79. Its country charm and sweet apple pies make for a pleasant stop. The PCT trailhead is at Scissors Crossing on CA 78, just east of CR S2. Parking is available across from the stop sign in the small dirt turnout on the east side of S2.

It is recommended to leave a second car at Barrel Springs and shuttle back to the Scissors Crossing trailhead. To reach Barrel Springs, take CR S2 north, and turn right (east) on CR S22 (also known as Montezuma Valley Road). Several shaded parking spots are available in a dirt pullout at the trail intersection. Do not leave valuables in your car since parking areas are rather isolated.

Overview

Devoid of water and stretching 23.1 miles one-way, this section of the Pacific Coast Trail is one of the longest and driest hikes in San Diego County. Unless you are in top physical shape and are prepared to carry at least five liters of water, it is best not to attempt this hike.

The long distance and difficult grades exacerbate the punishing temperatures, which sometimes exceed 100 degrees in summer. The only recommended season to attempt this hike is in winter, when daytime temperatures are generally in the seventies; Those overnighting should plan accordingly, since temperatures at higher elevations can drop below freezing this time of year. Be sure to leave Fido at home as burnt paws, snake bites, and dehydration may occur on desert hikes.

The largest state park in California, Anza-Borrego Desert State Park is home to several magnificent hikes and desert wildflowers that bloom in spring. Unfortunately, none of these notable hikes connects with the PCT. However, if you need a refreshing escape from the desert heat, or want to combine this hike with something more picturesque, visit nearby Maidenhair Falls. The seasonal 20-foot waterfall passes through Hellhole Canyon and begins just east of where this profiled hike ends.

Undoubtedly, anyone who wants to experience a sense of accomplishment by trekking across a desert stretch of the PCT will appreciate this hike. Beginning from Anza-Borrego Desert, the trail gradually climbs more than 2,000 feet, along the shadeless slopes of Grapevine Mountain. Agave stalks pepper the southwest flank, uncannily reminiscent of the Truffula Trees from Dr. Seuss's *The Lorax*.

In April and May, ocotillo shrubs bloom with scarlet flowers while beavertail cacti sprout pink petals from their spiny pads. Many switchbacks offer views of San Felipe Valley, with intermittent drops into dry furrows. Unfortunately, the paralleling County Road S2 is somewhat of an eyesore until it finally vanishes at the halfway point. Here begins the northeast ascent of the San Felipe Hills. The final stretch (or midway point for those who are doing a there-and-back) to Barrel Springs includes a downgrade through chaparral slopes and a brief portion of Hoover Canyon. The beauty and diversity of the last mile before County Road S22, lined with live oaks and grasslands, is the ultimate reward for this grueling hike.

The essential thing to bring on this hike is water. The arduous course was originally intended to pass through the Volcan Mountains. Rather than battle property owners, the U.S. Forest Service ran the PCT east of CR S2, through the dry San Felipe Hills, rather than through the pine-shaded Volcan Mountains to the west. As a result, this 23.1-mile desert trek veers sharply east and west, and can be dangerous because of the heat, isolation, length, and lack of water.

| Sunset near Barrel Springs

In Detail

From CA 78, begin at the PCT post, one of only three markers during this entire hike. Immediately, the trail ascends north through the cactus-strewn hills of San Felipe. This gateway into Anza-Borrego Desert State Park is dotted with barrel cactus, teddybear cactus, and agave stalks. At the half-mile mark, the trail begins to climb the southwest saddle of Grapevine Mountain. The switchbacks seem relentless, continually zigzagging east and west for 2 miles. This will be the last view of ocotillo shrubs, commonly

to reach this point. In the spring, a variety of wildflowers bloom, including Indian paintbrush, wild onion, and golden coreopsis. Agave stalks, some 10 feet high, cover the slopes.

Perhaps the most breathtaking view comes at 8 miles, where pink boulders form platforms high above San Felipe Valley. The aroma of sage fills the air, and manzanitas form a distant backdrop. Just short of 9 miles, a metal gate opens into a greener landscape. Juniper and scrub oak give way to a flat-bottomed wash that joins the trail and then bends to the left. The trail ascends westward, then eastward again before passing a small valley where camping might be possible.

Those who plan on camping at the midway point to Barrel Springs should continue to the crest at 13.3 miles, where land has been cleared. Now at 3,573 feet, the trail crosses an old jeep road and opens onto another gate and water cache. The San Diego Sierra Club has left a first-aid kit and, at the time of this writing, more than 50 gallons of water. The club restocks this heavenly gift throughout the spring peak-hiking season, though there are no guarantees that the bottles will be full. Desperate hikers may head 0.9 miles east (right) from here along a spur trail for additional water. A man named "Richard" allows travelers onto his Grapevine Canyon property to share his water.

That path creates the only trail fork on this entire hike. Continue on the PCT, now climbing the east shoulder of the San Felipe Hills. Yarrow, nightshade, and desert mallow add splashes of color in spring to the otherwise-drab terrain. Black beetles waddle into the sun while horned lizards dart under hot rocks. Cactus gives way to enormous groves of white-flowered chamise on the slopes.

The approach to the trail's fourth gate

called candlewood because the blossoms resemble flames. The flowers can also be fermented to produce wine.

As the grade increases and the sun scorches, you cannot help but notice the emerald valley framing the San Felipe Creek to the distant southwest. Near 3 miles, the switchbacks briefly subside as the trail dips into a series of washes. Throughout the climb, the PCT traverses such gullies, which contain water only during a deluge.

The rolling hills of San Felipe offer a pleasant view despite the effort required

| Horned lizard

allows an incredible view of the trail just traversed, no more than a thin line snaking through the mountain. Continue northeast into thick chaparral, still ascending to 4,395 feet. The route drops toward a steep ravine sprinkled with buttercups in season. For emergency shelter, a cave has been burrowed into the mountain at exactly 18 miles.

Finally, the long-awaited descent begins, with the trail winding nearly as much as during the beginning switchbacks. Entering a small section of Hoover Canyon, the trail sharply bends back and forth, dropping occasionally into furrows and gullies. The northeast view of Montezuma Valley offers the first sign of civilization. After crossing a wash, you'll pass through three gates. In the last mile before Barrel Springs, weary hikers are rewarded with an oak grove and a shaded valley that makes for a pleasant campsite.

In the absence of formal campground facilities, overnight hikers can enjoy a peaceful stay in this natural setting, with water just up ahead. Like most campsites, this is a fire-free zone. Fortunately, the refreshing conclusion comes in the cool water trough at Barrel Springs, where the trail meets County Road S22. From here, shuttle back to the trailhead at Scissors Crossing. Although not recommended, one can overnight in this area before hiking back 23 miles south on the PCT. For those who want to link this route to other neighboring trails, see Hikes 26 and 24.

Hike 26

Barrel Springs to Warner Springs

Distance: 16.86 miles round-trip or 8.43 miles with shuttle

Hiking time: 7–8 hours

Trail highlights: Meadows, trickling creek, Eagle Rock

Difficulty: ▲▲

Family friendly: ▲▲

Scenery: ▲▲▲

Solitude: ▲▲

Trail condition: ▲▲▲▲

Getting There

From Interstate 15, head east on CA 78, then turn left on CA 79 at Santa Ysabel and head north past Lake Henshaw. Turn right (east) onto County Road S2 (San Felipe Road) before veering left onto CR S22, also known as Montezuma Valley Road. The PCT trailhead is just beyond the 1-mile marker on this two-lane farm road. Several shaded parking spots are available in a dirt pullout across from the northbound trailhead.

To avoid a there-and-back hike, leave

| Canada Verde

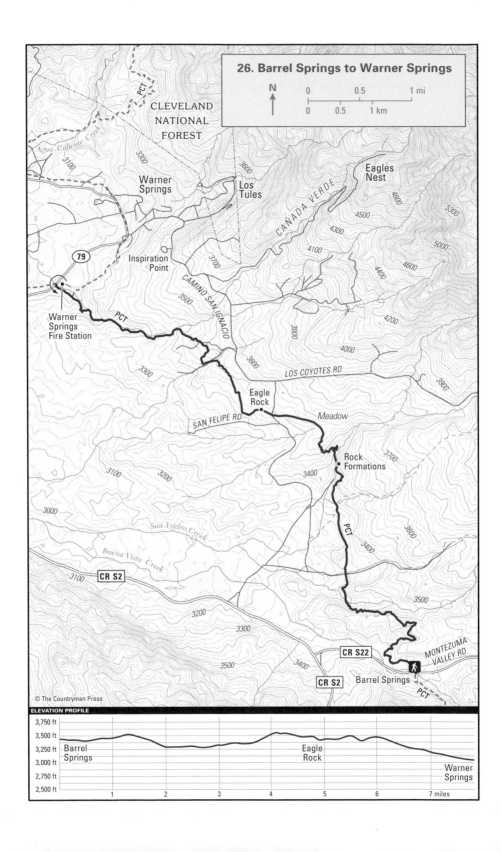

26. Barrel Springs to Warner Springs

N

| 0 | | 0.5 | | 1 mi |
| 0 | 0.5 | | 1 km | |

CLEVELAND
NATIONAL
FOREST

Eagles
Nest

Warner
Springs

Los
Tules

CAÑADA VERDE

Agua Caliente Creek

3100

3300

3600

4800

5300

4500

4300

4100

5000

4600

4400

4200

79

Inspiration
Point

CAMINO SAN IGNACIO

3700

3500

PCT

Warner
Springs
Fire Station

3300

3600

LOS COYOTES RD

4000

3900

Eagle
Rock

Meadow

SAN FELIPE RD

3700

Rock
Formations

3100

3200

3400

PCT

3600

3400

3000

San Ysidro Creek

Buena Vista Creek

CR S2

3100

3500

3200

3300

3500

3400

CR S22

MONTEZUMA
VALLEY RD

CR S2

Barrel Springs

PCT

© The Countryman Press

ELEVATION PROFILE

3,750 ft							
3,500 ft							
3,250 ft	Barrel				Eagle		
3,000 ft	Springs				Rock		
2,750 ft							Warner
2,500 ft							Springs
	1	2	3	4	5	6	7 miles

a second car parked across from Warner Springs Fire Station, located at 31049 CA 79. From here, shuttle back to the trailhead at Barrel Springs. Parking permits are not required.

GPS TRAILHEAD COORDINATES

UTM Zone	11S
Easting	538385
Northing	3675409
Latitude	N33.21691°
Longitude	W116.58809°

Overview

Slicing between County Road S22 and CA 79, this tranquil stretch of the Pacific Crest Trail offers diverse scenery. What begins as a canyon climb soon drops into meadows and open plains. San Ysidro Creek, which periodically parallels the trail, adds a refreshing touch to the somewhat dry terrain. After a brief uphill trek, hikers are rewarded with westward views stretching to Lake Henshaw.

The scenery dramatically changes in the final section (also the turnaround point) before Warner Springs, alternating between chaparral slopes and barren grasslands. The rangeland of Canada Verde, shaded with live oaks and cottonwoods, is the perfect place to camp for those heading north to Agua Caliente Creek. This trail can best be enjoyed in April, when California poppies adorn the fields.

Although Warner's Hot Springs (at the turnaround point) are no longer open to the public, they once served as a meeting place for Native Americans and immigrants who passed through the region. Named for Juan Jose Warner, who built Warner Springs Ranch in 1844, the town is famous for this historic landmark, where the first Butterfield Stagecoach stopped in 1858.

Until it filed for bankruptcy 2012, Warner Springs Ranch served as a luxury resort with golfing, horseback riding, tennis courts, and a spa. It also offered access to the hot springs that were discovered in 1795 during a Spanish expedition led by Fray Juan Mariner. New hot spring pools were constructed in 1922.

When in operation, the resort received resupply packages for PCT thru-hikers, but now it is suggested to have parcels shipped to the Warner Springs post office. At the time of this writing, there was talk of the Pala Band of Mission Indians purchasing the 2,500 acre resort, but legal battles have kept deals from moving forward. Perhaps one day, hikers can explore this historical treasure once again.

In Detail

The trek begins on a dirt trail at the 1-mile marker of Montezuma Valley Road (CR S22). After a metal cattle gate comes a fork in the trail. A series of PCT markers guides hikers to the left, past the "No Trespassing" sign posted by Vista Irrigation.

When spring flowers are in bloom, the trail introduces subtle hints of what lies ahead, including white forget-me-nots and blue phacelias. Entire slopes of lavender lupine dramatically contrast with the brittle needles of hot pink flowering cacti.

After following the base of a ridge, the trail climbs a small canyon scented with ginger and sage. In the spring, this area blushes with Indian paintbrush, western wallflowers, golden yarrows, and fiddleneck.

A switchback leads to a thick chaparral valley where stalks of Our Lord's Candle sprout. The trail gradually ascends before

| A shaded knoll of live oaks and cottonwoods

sinking into a peaceful grassland where engraved wooden posts mark the way. This
lovely meadow is overshadowed only by a
much larger one just beyond a ridge ahead.

At 3.5 miles, taupe fields suddenly yield
to the lush oaks of San Ysidro Creek. In
April and May, the creek flows along most of
the remainder of the hike, adding a pleasant

veer toward the old jeep road on the right. Beyond the creek, the steepest ascension of the hike begins up the ridge. Throughout this climb, patches of Canterbury bells and desert mallows contrast with the roots of dark manzanita trees.

Just beyond 4 miles, the trail bends and enters an open plain. California poppies scattered across this meadow are spectacular in spring. Also striking are the violet clusters of woolly blue curls, a flower once used by travelers to treat ulcers and alleviate pain.

Just before 5 miles, the trail forks left, away from a jeep trail that formerly was part of the PCT. Just beyond this split, note the large boulders known as Eagle Rock. The back side of this rock formation is shaped like a flying eagle. From here, a brief descent precedes a somewhat steep climb up a chamise-covered hillside.

Just before the 7-mile mark comes a highlight of the journey, Canada Verde. Emerald grass and wild flowers blanket this "Green Ravine." After crossing a sandy wash, the trail reaches a shaded knoll of live oaks and cottonwoods. The trail intermittently parallels the creek bed. After running along the well-vegetated canyon, the trail passes through several metal gates before reaching CA 79. Water is available here, at Warner Springs Fire Station.

Whether you're doing the hike in a single day or plan to stay in Warner Springs, head back the same way you came, concluding at the Barrel Springs trailhead on Montezuma Valley Road (CR S22). For a one-way hike, shuttle back by car along S2. Overnight camping is available at Indian Flats Campground 7 miles north of Warner Springs. For those wanting to continue on the PCT from Warner Springs to Agua Caliente Creek (see Hike 27), follow the trail under the concrete bridge and continue north.

bonus of both sight and sound. Just before the creek crossing, a grove lined by a stone wall offers the ideal spot for a break.

Be sure to cross the creek rather than

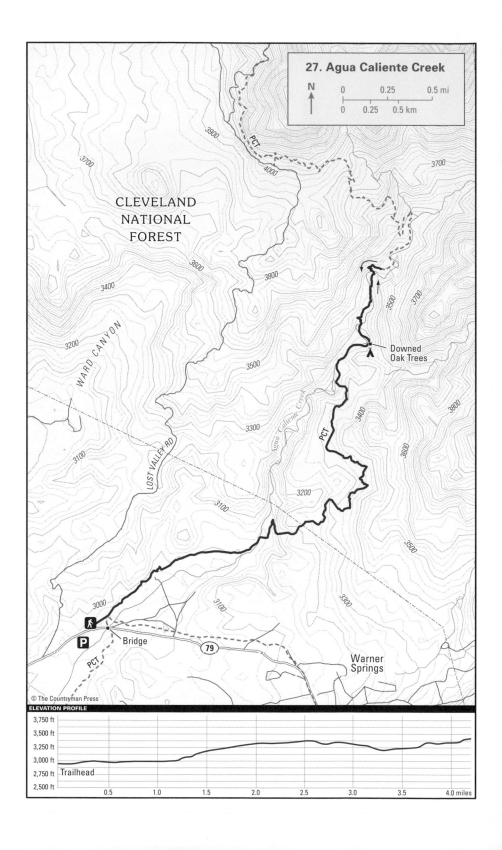

27. Agua Caliente Creek

N

| 0 | 0.25 | 0.5 mi |

| 0 | 0.25 | 0.5 km |

CLEVELAND
NATIONAL
FOREST

3900

4000

PCT

3700

3700

3800

3600

3400

3500

3800

3700

3500

Downed
Oak Trees

WARD CANYON

3200

3500

3400

3800

Agua Caliente Creek

PCT

3300

3600

3100

3200

3100

3500

LOST VALLEY RD

3100

3300

3000

79

Warner
Springs

Bridge

PCT

© The Countryman Press

ELEVATION PROFILE

| 3,750 ft |
| 3,500 ft |
| 3,250 ft |
| 3,000 ft |
| 2,750 ft | Trailhead |
| 2,500 ft |

| 0.5 | 1.0 | 1.5 | 2.0 | 2.5 | 3.0 | 3.5 | 4.0 miles |

Hike 27

Agua Caliente Creek

Distance: 8 miles round-trip

Hiking time: 4 hours

Trail highlights: Meandering trail, canyon view, interweaving creek

Difficulty: ▲▲▲

Family friendly: ▲▲

Scenery: ▲▲▲

Solitude: ▲▲▲▲

Trail condition: ▲▲▲

Getting There

From Interstate I-15, exit onto CA 78, and turn left (north) onto CA 79 at Santa Ysabel. Follow CA 79 north toward Warner Springs. Watch for the Agua Caliente Creek Bridge at mile 36.6. If you reach the Warner Springs Glider Port, you have gone too far. The trailhead, below the road, can be difficult to find. On the south side of the road is a dirt turnout with parking for five cars. Parking permits are not required.

GPS TRAILHEAD COORDINATES

UTM Zone	11S
Easting	531994
Northing	3683332
Latitude	N33.28857°
Longitude	W116.65639°

Overview

This scenic slice of the Pacific Crest Trail crisscrosses Agua Caliente Creek, past towering trees and shaded campsites. A mile into the trek, the sounds of urban chatter surrender to nature's peace. Flatlands and sparse vegetation near Warner Springs soon give way to cottonwoods scattered

| Cholla cactus near Agua Caliente Creek

| Autumn trees of gold

throughout a canyon. This sandy trail gradually ascends past live oaks, sycamores, and alders. Sun-bleached yucca, cacti, and claret-colored boulders sporadically brighten the chaparral landscape.

Throughout the hike, the PCT and Agua Caliente Creek weave together, adding vitality to the landscape. Conditions vary by season. During the winter, heavy rains can create unsafe conditions along the water's edge. Summer is dry and hot, and the creek flows only at higher elevations. Late autumn, when the air is crisp and the trees are still blushing bright red and gold, is an optimum time for this hike. Although the creek stops flowing in this profiled area from mid-spring to early fall, it still shows signs of life through its intermittent trickling waters.

At times, hikers may mistake the dry creek bed for the trail. Follow the PCT wooden-post markers to avoid wandering off course. Although relatively arid, this out-and-back hike gains richness from the canyon views.

In Detail

From the parking area, head north toward the metal gate where the PCT crosses under Agua Caliente Creek Bridge. Follow the PCT posts along the creek bed toward a cylindrical water tower. You'll be paralleling the California Riding and Hiking Trail, which is clearly wider than the PCT. The hike actually begins on Warner Ranch Resort property, which officially closed in 2012 due to bankruptcy. Hikers are permitted to enter the property to access the PCT.

Proceed upstream along the dirt trail. Minutes into the hike, a faded wooden sign marks side trails that offer the possibility of overnight treks to Lost Valley Road and the Riverside County line farther north. As if

| 281 Fall colors on the trail

choreographed by nature, the trail and creek begin to curve in parallel formation. Sun-baked soil and low scrub brush soon give way to canopies of willow, sycamore, and cottonwood trees that periodically shade the trail. An enormous oak tree spreads its branches over the path.

Just beyond the first mile is the hike's only developed (barely) campsite. It consists of a wooden table and a rusty barbecue grill. There may be several more appealing creekside locations farther ahead. Soon thereafter, the trail begins to ascend northeast, bypassing Ward Canyon.

For the next 2 miles, the trail snakes past towering rock formations as it coils back and forth over the creek bed. Like a patchwork fortress, the stone walls range from deep ochre to moss-covered limestone. The stone-strewn path crosses the shallow creek several times.

Another shaded resting spot comes at around 3.5 miles, where downed oak trees create an open space in the grove. With the creek to the left, this break in the path provides sublime solitude. Just before 4 miles, again cross Agua Caliente Creek, where water flows year-round. You will have now entered into Cleveland National Forest.

As the PCT breaks away from the creek (just beyond 4 miles), turn around and retrace your steps to the trailhead. Those who continue farther north toward Pine Mountain and Indian Flats should be aware that the trek becomes steep, less impressive, and dangerous after heavy rainfall.

Hikers will surely be amazed by how different the scenery looks on the return leg as their new perspective reveals the valleys below. Especially in autumn, the mustard-hued vistas and rolling hills are particularly breathtaking.

| Side trip to freshwater pools near Caramba Overlook |

PART III

San Jacinto Wilderness, San Gorgonio Wilderness, and San Bernardino Forest

| Scarlet Bugler |

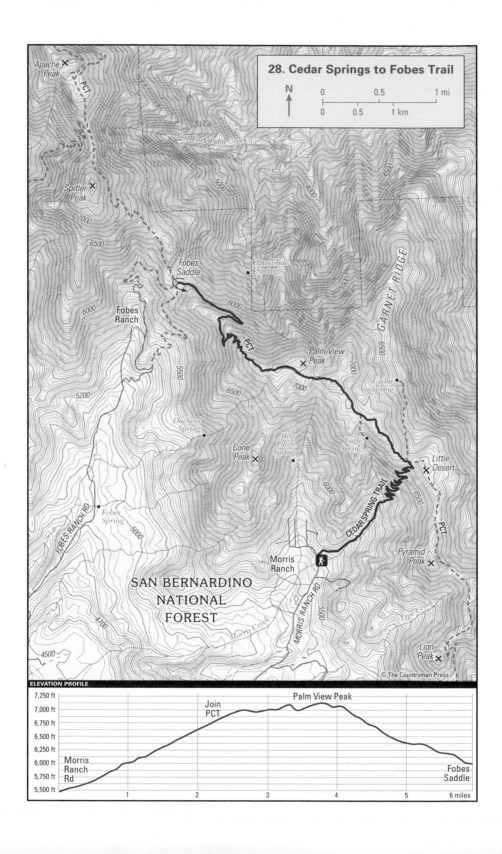

28. Cedar Springs to Fobes Trail

N

| 0 | | 0.5 | | 1 mi |
| 0 | 0.5 | | 1 km | |

Apache Peak ✕

PCT

West Fork Palm Creek

Spitler Peak ✕

7000

6500

6000

5200

Fobes Ranch

Fobes Saddle

5500

Duchess Spring

5000

Fobes Spring

Cone Peak ✕

SAN BERNARDINO
NATIONAL
FOREST

4700

Morris Creek

4500

FOBES RANCH RD

5000

6500

6000

6500

7000

PCT

Palm View Peak ✕

Landslide Spring

GARNET RIDGE

5500

6000

6000

Cedar Spring

Hop Patch Spring

Eagle Spring

CEDAR SPRING TRAIL

Little Desert ✕

6500

PCT

Morris Ranch

MORRIS RANCH RD

5500

Pyramid Peak ✕

Piper Creek

Lion Peak ✕

© The Countryman Press

ELEVATION PROFILE

Palm View Peak

Join PCT

Morris Ranch Rd

Fobes Saddle

	7,250 ft
	7,000 ft
	6,750 ft
	6,500 ft
	6,250 ft
	6,000 ft
	5,750 ft
	5,500 ft

1   2   3   4   5   6 miles

Hike 28

Cedar Springs to Fobes Trail

Distance: 12 miles round-trip or 7.5 miles via Fobes Trail	
Hiking time: 6 hours	
Trail highlights: Lake views, rolling hills, forest landscape	
Difficulty: ▲▲▲	
Family friendly: Not recommended	
Scenery: ▲▲▲▲	
Solitude: ▲▲▲	
Trail condition: ▲▲▲	

GPS TRAILHEAD COORDINATES	
UTM Zone	11S
Easting	537768
Northing	3723872
Latitude	N33.65404°
Longitude	W116.59267°

Getting There

From Interstate 215 south of Riverside, exit onto CA 74 east (Exit 15). After approximately 40 miles, turn left onto Morris Ranch Road. After 5 miles, you'll see the wooden gate marking the trailhead for the Cedar Springs Trail on the right. Parking is available on the road shoulder.

For those who prefer to shuttle back to the Cedar Springs Trail trailhead, park a second car at the Fobes Trail parking area, accessed by way of Fobes Ranch Road off CA 74. A National Forest Adventure Pass is required to park in both areas.

Overview

For the motivated hiker, the highlight of Cedar Springs Trail may be the 4-mile ascent to the Pacific Crest Trail. In the initial climb, the trail forsakes a desert landscape to enter forest terrain.

Unlike Anza-Borrego Desert, the San Bernardino Mountains are home to tree species such as white fir and five types of pine. This area showcases more than 2,000 species of plants, 267 species of birds, 55 species of reptiles, and 75 species of mammals—the latter including mountain lions, raccoons, jackrabbits, and bighorn sheep.

The trail is easily accessible from CA 74. Lake views, rolling hills, and forests are a few of the draws, but be prepared to pay heavily for the natural beauty: The heat can make the climb brutal during the summer months, and it can be difficult to navigate in winter, when snow envelopes the trail.

Still, this hike is the perfect launching point for exploration of the San Bernardino National Forest and the San Jacinto Wilderness. (Sadly, 27,531 acres of wilderness were scorched during the July 2013 Moun-

| Greener days near Fobes Trail

tain Fire near Idyllwild, which was caused by electrical equipment failure.) For those who want to experience more of the PCT across this region, Hikes 28 to 34 can be linked together consecutively, allowing for several overnight hikes. Alternatively, they can also be traveled independently as there-and-back hikes.

In Detail

To hike from Cedar Springs to Fobes Trail, park along Morris Ranch Road off CA 74. Pass through the wooden gate marked "Cedar Springs Trail." There's a water tower beyond the trailhead and a sign directing hikers onto the narrow dirt trail. After going through

a second gate, the route parallels a creek bed before gray rock slabs envelop the trail.

You'll pass through another metal gate that opens onto a grassy field. Be sure to close the gates behind you. A small picnic area provides the perfect spot for a breather after the initial ascent. After that, the trail narrows and climbs through dry slopes of agave, beavertail cactus, and chaparral. If you look back, you can see inviting Morris Creek sparkling in the distance. Just before 3 miles, the Cedar Springs Trail meets the PCT.

Head north (left) on the PCT, where California poppies bloom in clusters in season. Continue on the now–pink granite path, lined by manzanita shrubs. The sights of Garnet Ridge to the north and the rolling

| Towering pines

hills of San Bernardino National Forest to the east compete with the distant lake views.

During spring, Indian paintbrush and brittlebush provide color among the white firs and Coulter pines. As you approach 4 miles, shrubs that resemble broccoli grow over the trail, making it difficult to navigate. Continue north on the PCT. Scarlet buglers and spruce trees decorate the route, which overlooks Lake Hemet to the west. Next, the trail dips into forest area.

At 6 miles, the PCT levels out and intersects Fobes Trail coming up from the west (left). This is the turnaround point for this hike. From here, head back 6 miles to the trailhead for the Cedar Springs Trail. For those who prefer to shuttle back, leave a second car at the base of Fobes Trail, located 1.5 miles from the PCT. This route can be accessed by way of CA 74 to Fobes Ranch Road.

If you want to spend more time here, the saddle at the 6-mile point allows for primitive camping, permitted within the San Jacinto Wilderness. Free permits, required for both day hiking and overnight camping, can be obtained from the Idyllwild Ranger Station at the intersection of Highway 243 and Pine Crest Drive. A limited number of campers are allowed in this wilderness area at any given time, so get your free permit well in advance of your trip. Permit applications are also available at www.fsva.org.

To extend your adventure, continue north on the PCT by following Hike 29.

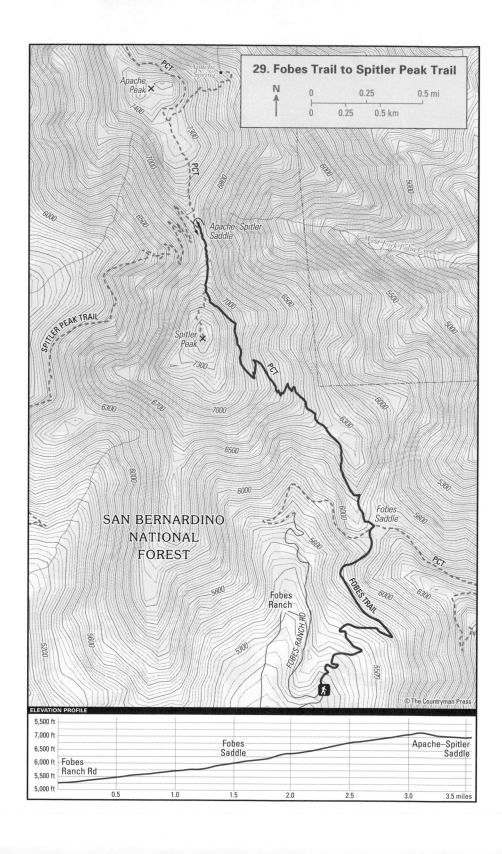

29. Fobes Trail to Spitler Peak Trail

N

| 0 | 0.25 | 0.5 mi |
| 0 | 0.25 | 0.5 km |

Apache Peak ✕

Apache Spring

PCT

7400

7300

7000

6500

6000

PCT

Apache–Spitler Saddle

West Fork Palm Creek

6000

5000

SPITLER PEAK TRAIL

Spitler Peak ✕

7000

7300

6300

6700

7000

6500

6000

5800

5300

5200

5600

SAN BERNARDINO NATIONAL FOREST

5600

6000

6500

6300

PCT

Fobes Saddle

5900

5300

5500

6000

FOBES TRAIL

Fobes Ranch

FOBES RANCH RD

© The Countryman Press

ELEVATION PROFILE

5,500 ft						
7,000 ft						
6,500 ft			Fobes Saddle		Apache–Spitler Saddle	
6,000 ft	Fobes Ranch Rd					
5,500 ft						
5,000 ft						

| 0.5 | 1.0 | 1.5 | 2.0 | 2.5 | 3.0 | 3.5 miles |

Hike 29

Fobes Trail to Spitler Peak Trail

Distance: 7 miles round-trip or 8.5 miles
   via Spitler Peak Trail

Hiking time: 4 hours

Trail highlights: Views of Spitler Peak,
   variety of ecosystems

Difficulty: ▲▲▲

Family friendly: Not recommended

Scenery: ▲▲▲

Solitude: ▲▲▲

Trail condition: ▲▲▲

Getting There

From Interstate 215 south of Riverside, exit onto CA 74 east (Exit 15). After entering the San Bernardino National Forest, continue 2 miles past Lake Hemet, and turn left onto Fobes Ranch Road, marked by a wooden sign on a fence. After nearly 3.5 miles, turn right at the signed fork and continue 0.5 miles to the trailhead. Parking is available for five vehicles, with additional parking farther up the road.

For those who want to shuttle back to Fobes Trail (rather than hike), park a second car at the Spitler Peak parking area. It can be reached by heading east on the 74 to Apple Canyon Road, just before Lake Hemet. Turn left, pass Apple Canyon camping area, and follow the road 2 miles to the parking area just south of the Spitler Peak Trail. Hiking from Fobes parking area to Spitler Peak parking area (via the PCT) will result in an

8.5-mile trek. A National Forest Adventure Pass is required for parking in this area.

This entry was written prior to the 2013 Mountain Fire that destroyed 23 structures, 7 homes, and 43 square miles east of Apple Canyon. The two-week blaze raged across the southern portion of the San Jacinto Wilderness along the Desert Divide.

To experience more of the PCT across this region, Hikes 28 to 34 can be linked

| Entering San Jacinto Wilderness

together consecutively, allowing for several overnight hikes. Camping permits are available up to 90 days in advance from the Idyllwild Ranger Station and can be obtained by calling 951-659-2117 or 909-382-2921. Permit applications are available at www.fsva.org.

GPS TRAILHEAD COORDINATES

UTM Zone	11S
Easting	536155
Northing	3727853
Latitude	N33.69000°
Longitude	W116.60990°

Overview

This route passes through several climate zones. You'll see everything from chaparral and oak to pine and granite. Keep in mind that the landscape may take decades to fully recover from the destruction of the 2013 Mountain Fire. Nearly every step of this trek offers a spectacular view, including those of Lake Hemet and Spitler Peak. Adventure-seekers can take the spur trail to Spitler Peak—elevation 7,360 feet—which offers views that span from the ocean to the desert. Bring plenty of water; conditions can be brutally hot in summer.

In Detail

From the parking area, climb 1.5 miles north on Fobes Trail. Upon reaching Fobes Saddle, turn left onto the Pacific Crest Trail. Then comes a steep grade north, climbing 1,000 feet in just over a mile.

Although a sign marks the entrance into San Jacinto Wilderness, the forest has already announced itself with its smell of ponderosa pines, white firs, and Jeffrey pines. Switchbacks relentlessly clamber up the ridge past charred remnants of other wildfires, including the 2003 Cedar Fire, which caused damage to surrounding canyons.

Color shows in the form of scarlet buglers and blue-eyed grass in spring. To the east lies the Agua Caliente Indian Reservation, the only sign of civilization you'll see on the hike. Along the trail are rust-hued rocks and gray granite slabs swirled with black and white stripes.

For a side adventure to Spitler Peak, turn left off the PCT at the cairn. This spur trail is located at the trail's highest elevation point, northeast of the summit. The Spitler Peak turn off will take you 1 mile (one-way) up a ridge to Spitler Peak. You may have to do a bit of scrambling to get there, but you'll be rewarded with 360-degree views of Palm Springs and the Coachella Valley. The top of the mountain is exquisitely forested with yellow pines. From here, return back to the PCT to continue the hike.

Whether you venture to Spitler Peak or not, from this spur trail turnoff, you'll eventually continue north on the PCT. Hikers will encounter a cool forest of oak, maple, and pine. To reach the turnaround point of the trek, follow the PCT until it meets Spitler Peak Trail, which approaches from the left (west).

For those seeking a one-way route, have a second car waiting at the trailhead for the Spitler Peak Trail off of Apple Canyon Road. To reach this parking area, leave the PCT and hike 5 miles west down Spitler Peak Trail. The hike through desert chaparral to the Spitler Peak parking area brings you down to 4,950 feet in elevation. The trail from one parking area to the other, by way of the PCT, will make your hike 8.5 miles.

For a there-and-back hike (turning around at the PCT–Spitler Peak Trail junction), return 3.5 miles south along the PCT to your starting point at Fobes Trail parking area. This round-trip option will make your hike 7 miles total.

| Climbing toward Spitler Peak

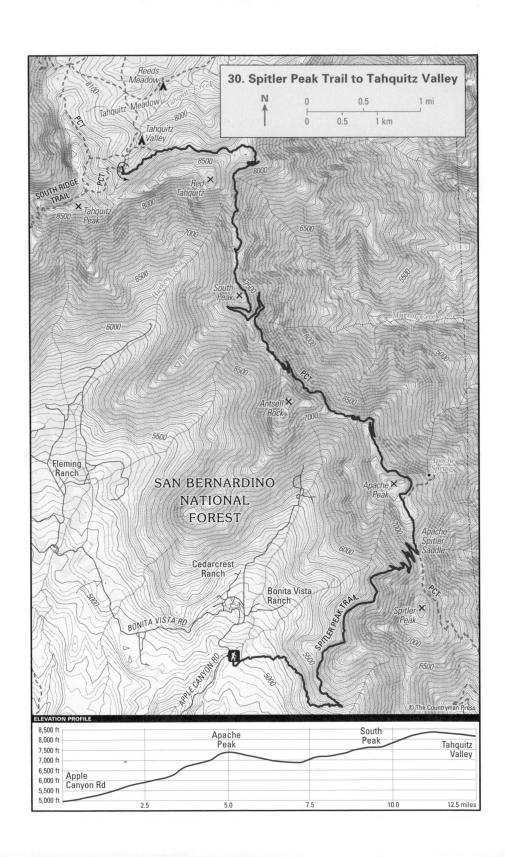

N

| 0 | | 0.5 | | 1 mi |
| 0 | 0.5 | | 1 km | |

Reeds
Meadow

Tahquitz Meadow

Tahquitz
Valley

PCT

8100

8000

8500

8000

Red
Tahquitz ✕

SOUTH RIDGE
TRAIL

PCT

✕ Tahquitz
Peak

8500

8000

7000

6500

Hacker Creek

6000

5500

Fleming
Ranch

SAN BERNARDINO
NATIONAL
FOREST

South
Peak ✕

7500

6500

Antsell
Rock ✕

7000

7500

8000

6500

Tahquitz Creek

6500

6000

PCT

Murray Creek

5500

5000

5500

6000

6500

Apache
Spring ■

Apache ✕
Peak

7000

Apache-
Spitler
Saddle

PCT

Cedarcrest
Ranch

Bonita Vista
Ranch

SPITLER PEAK TRAIL

6000

Spitler ✕
Peak

7000

6500

BONITA VISTA RD

5000

5500

APPLE CANYON RD

5500

© The Countryman Press

ELEVATION PROFILE

8,500 ft				South		
8,000 ft			Apache	Peak		
7,500 ft			Peak			
7,000 ft						Tahquitz
6,500 ft						Valley
6,000 ft						
5,500 ft	Apple					
5,000 ft	Canyon Rd					

2.5   5.0   7.5   10.0   12.5 miles

Hike 30

Spitler Peak Trail to Tahquitz Valley

Distance: 24 miles round-trip or 16.7 miles via South Ridge

Hiking time: 12 hours

Trail highlights: Flowing water, nearby swimming hole and waterfalls

Difficulty: ▲▲▲▲

Family friendly: Not recommended

Scenery: ▲▲▲▲

Solitude: ▲▲▲▲

Trail condition: ▲▲▲

GPS TRAILHEAD COORDINATES

UTM Zone	11S
Easting	534971
Northing	3730066
Latitude	N33.71000°
Longitude	W116.62259°

Getting There

From Interstate 215 south of Riverside, exit onto CA 74 east (Exit 15). After entering the San Bernardino National Forest, head toward Lake Hemet, and turn left onto Apple Canyon Road at the sign for Hurkey Creek Park. Continue nearly 3 miles until you reach the parking area for Spitler Peak Trail. The trailhead is just north of the parking turnout.

For a one-way hike, park a second car at the South Ridge Trail parking area. To reach the South Ridge Trail trailhead, take CA 74 east to 243 north toward Idyllwild. Turn right on Saunders Meadow Road, left on Pine Avenue, and right on Tahquitz View Drive. Finally, turn right onto South Ridge Road (Forest Route 5S11). Parked vehicles must display a National Forest Adventure Pass.

Overview

One of the most challenging hikes in the region, this 12-mile (one-way) trail is also one of the most rewarding. It offers the best of the San Jacinto Wilderness, from a variety of landscapes to a cool stream. This hike description was written prior to the 2013 Mountain Fire that burned sections of Garner Valley, Mountain Center, Mount San Jacinto State Park, and the San Bernardino National Forest and wilderness areas. Starting in desert terrain, the hike features valleys, oak forests, and spring wildflowers. Crimson penstemon drapes entire slopes while fir and pine aromas perfume the air. Steep ridge switchbacks and white boulders give way to a sandy "terrace," an ideal spot for lunch. The greatest joy of this challenge comes at the turnaround point, a tributary of Tahquitz Creek.

From here, hikers can return southbound on the PCT to Spitler Peak Trail parking area, making the hike 24 miles round trip. For a one-way route (which involves shuttling back to the Spitler Peak parking area via CA 243 and CA 74) hikers can descend 4 miles along South Ridge Trail to the parking area, making the hike a total of 16.7 miles.

To experience a greater section of the PCT across this region, Hikes 28 to 34 can be linked together consecutively, allowing for several overnight hikes. Camping permits are available up to 90 days in advance from the Idyllwild Ranger Station and can be obtained by calling 951-659-2117 or 909-382-2921. Permit applications are available at www.fsva.org.

In Detail

Begin at the marked post at the north end of the Spitler Peak Trail parking area. The climb from the trailhead to the Pacific Crest Trail junction is gradual in the first 3 miles. Then come 2 miles of switchbacks, winding past yucca and cactus-covered slopes, before you reach the PCT. After this initial 5-mile climb, turn left (north) onto the PCT at the Apache–Spitler saddle.

Desert and forest landscapes collide in this transitional stretch of the PCT. In spring, larkspurs and scarlet buglers beautifully grace the trail, with purple blossoms bathing entire hillsides. Hikers may see hummingbirds, squirrels, and butterflies.

Bending slightly east, the trail enters a cluster of manzanitas before passing a sign announcing the entrance to San Jacinto Wilderness. A spur trail at 5.5 miles breaks off to the right, taking you to Apache Spring, half a mile to the east, where water is seasonally available. It usually runs dry in summer.

Continue climbing north along the PCT, now on the eastern shoulder of Apache Peak. This area blooms with white phlox and Indian paintbrush in spring. Just beyond the Coachella Valley lies Joshua Tree National Park.

The trail passes gray slate boulders, and soon opens toward the ominous mountains that tower ahead. Against the backdrop of the majestic peaks, begin the grueling ascent to 8,000 feet.

Continue along the steep ridge past a small clearing at the 7-mile mark, where camping is available. Near Antsell Rock, to

| Camping near Reeds Meadow. Photo by Justin McChesney

| Trekking toward Tahquitz Valley

the west, shade can create ice patches in winter and early spring. Traverse the pink-granite terrain, switching back several times, to enter a forest of lodgepole pines and white fir.

The forest gives way to catclaw shrubs, their thorns often leaving painful proof that you are in nature's domain. Leveling out slightly, the trail offers views of Murray Canyon to the east. Then the PCT cuts back into the forest, past purple wildflowers and Jeffery pines.

As you climb farther north, sadly the blanket of smog over Los Angeles County can be seen in the distance. Be careful near 10 miles, where poison oak grows trailside. The trail bends past white rock slabs and then spills onto a beach-like clearing. This is an inviting spot for a break before the final leg of the "out" part of the journey.

Follow the PCT as it parallels a massive rock wall before winding and then descending. Just before this segment of the trek ends, the trail meets a south tributary of Tahquitz Creek. Here, water usually flows year-round, though you have to purify it be-

fore drinking. This secluded area, although primitive, is adequate for tranquil camping.

Flat rocks make a decent spot to enjoy a picnic or cool-off in the shade. Cross the stream to reach the Tahquitz Valley, where designated camping is available 0.8 miles north. Additional campsites, marked by yellow posts, are available 1.5 miles northeast of Tahquitz Valley at Reeds Meadow. Unpurified stream water can also be found here.

If time allows, take a side trip from Reeds Meadow 3.5 miles (one-way) to Caramba Overlook, where you can cool off in freshwater pools and waterfalls. The trek through Reeds Meadow is especially beautiful because of all the ferns throughout the forest.

To complete the hike from Tahquitz Valley, return 12 miles south on the PCT to the trailhead for the Spitler Peak Trail. For those who plan to shuttle back to Spitler Peak Trail, leave the PCT and head left on South Ridge Trail. This 4-mile trail passes Tahquitz Peak, ending at the South Ridge parking area. From here, shuttle back by way of CA 243 and CA 74 to the Spitler Peak Trail parking area, where the hike began.

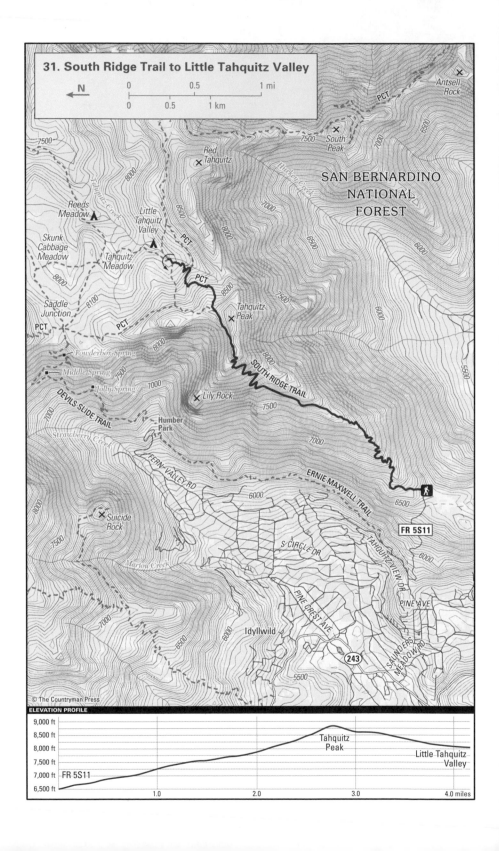

31. South Ridge Trail to Little Tahquitz Valley

N

| 0 | | 0.5 | | 1 mi |
| 0 | 0.5 | | 1 km | |

Antsell
Rock

PCT

South
Peak

Red
Tahquitz

SAN BERNARDINO
NATIONAL
FOREST

Tahquitz Creek

7500

8000

8500

8000

7000

6500

6000

5500

Reeds
Meadow

Little
Tahquitz
Valley

PCT

Skunk
Cabbage
Meadow

Tahquitz
Meadow

PCT

8000

8100

Tahquitz
Peak

Saddle
Junction

PCT

PCT

PCT

Powderbox Spring

SOUTH RIDGE TRAIL

8000

Middle Spring

7500

Jolly Spring

7000

Lily Rock

7500

7000

DEVILS SLIDE TRAIL

Strawberry Creek

Humber
Park

7000

ERNIE MAXWELL TRAIL

6500

FERN VALLEY RD

6000

6500

Suicide
Rock

7500

FR 5S11

Marion Creek

S CIRCLE DR

TAHQUITZVIEW DR

PINE AVE

6000

7000

PINE CREST AVE

Idyllwild

6000

243

SAUNDERS MEADOW RD

5500

© The Countryman Press

ELEVATION PROFILE

9,000 ft				
8,500 ft			Tahquitz	
8,000 ft			Peak	Little Tahquitz
7,500 ft				Valley
7,000 ft	FR 5S11			
6,500 ft				
	1.0	2.0	3.0	4.0 miles

Hike 31

South Ridge Trail to Little Tahquitz Valley

Distance: 9.6 miles round-trip	
Hiking time: 4–5 hours	
Trail highlights: Strawberry Valley views, western white pines	
Difficulty: ▲▲▲	
Family friendly: ▲	
Scenery: ▲▲	
Solitude: ▲▲▲	
Trail condition: ▲▲▲	

Getting There

From Interstate 215 south of Riverside, exit onto CA 74 east (Exit 15). After entering the San Bernardino National Forest, turn left onto CA 243 toward Idyllwild. At Saunders Meadow Road (after Marian View Drive), turn right. Turn left onto Pine Avenue, then right onto Tahquitz View Drive. Lastly, turn right onto South Ridge Road (Forest Route 5S11), and continue until you reach the trailhead. You'll need a National Forest Adventure Pass to park here.

GPS TRAILHEAD COORDINATES

UTM Zone	11S
Easting	531060
Northing	3735877
Latitude	N33.76253°
Longitude	W116.66460°

Overview

Unlike some lengthier PCT sections in this region, this hike only covers 0.8 mile on the Pacific Crest Trail, with the rest of the trek traveling along South Ridge Trail to Little Tahquitz Valley. The best way to enjoy this PCT stretch is by linking it to Hikes 30 and 32 on either end. For those with more time, Hikes 28 to 34 can be linked together consecutively, allowing for several overnight hikes.

Otherwise, an out-and-back hike will need to begin and end from the parking area for the South Ridge Trail. After 3.6 miles of switchbacks on South Ridge Trail, hikers can continue toward the PCT or attempt a side trip to the Tahquitz Peak summit, a 0.5-mile climb (one-way). Hikers may choose to explore this historic fire lookout on Tahquitz Peak before continuing 0.4 miles to the PCT junction. From here, continue right (northeast) toward Little Tahquitz Valley. This brief section of the PCT passes granite boulders, gravel slopes, and a pine forest.

Overnight hikers might enjoy a side trip from Tahquitz Valley–through Reeds Meadow –to Caramba Overlook. This 4.4 mile (one-way) addition passes through a fern valley toward a swimming hole and waterfall.

In Detail

This out-and-back trip to Little Tahquitz Valley travels along South Ridge Trail and allows for viewing of Tahquitz Peak and camping at Tahquitz Valley. From the South

| Indian paintbrush

| Caramba Overlook

Ridge Trail parking area, begin a steep, 2,000-foot ascent toward the PCT, past oak, fir, and pine trees. Just beyond the first mile on South Ridge Trail are south-facing views of Lake Hemet, Garner Valley, and Thomas Mountain. Some views may show signs of the 2013 Mountain Fire that burned the high ridges east of Idyllwild. Tight switchbacks continue for a total of 3.6 miles, stopping just before the spur trail to Tahquitz Peak.

Those who want bonus views can turn right onto the Tahquitz Peak Trail. This 0.5-mile hike to the summit involves a series of steep switchbacks that give way to a look-out tower at 8,846 feet, providing views of Strawberry Valley.

For those who hiked to the peak, head back down Tahquitz Peak Trail, and turn right onto South Ridge Trail. From here, continue 0.4 miles on South Ridge Trail until the route intersects the PCT. Now, having completed the 4-mile climb on South Ridge Trail, take the right fork at the PCT intersection that leads to Little Tahquitz Valley.

During this 0.8-mile (one-way) stretch on the PCT to the valley, you will pass a series of shrubs and western white pines. In spring, patches of Indian paintbrush splash

color among the white-sand clearings while woodpeckers tap overhead. Early-rising hikers may encounter deer, mourning doves, and black-tailed jackrabbits.

Switchbacks pass through an area of lodgepole pines, eaten away by mountain pine beetles. At the end of the 0.8-mile leg, you will come to a three-way junction; north leads to Reeds Meadow and Skunk Cabbage Meadow, east continues along the PCT (profiled in Hike 30), and southwest takes you back in the direction from which you came. Designated campsites, marked by yellow posts, are scattered just north of

this junction, in Tahquitz Valley. Remember to obtain a camping permit for this area from the Idyllwild Ranger Station.

To complete the hike, return 4.8 miles in the direction from which you came, along the PCT to the South Ridge Trail parking area. Hikers who camp overnight may choose to continue north on the PCT to Saddle Junction (see Hike 32).

Camping permits are available up to 90 days in advance from the Idyllwild Ranger Station and can be obtained by calling 951-659-2117 or 909-382-2921. Permit applications are available at www.fsva.org.

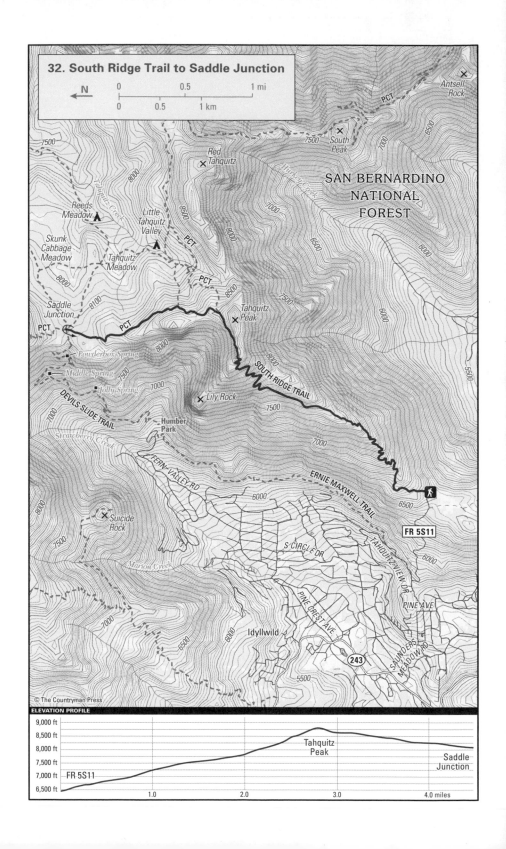

32. South Ridge Trail to Saddle Junction

N

| 0 | 0.5 | 1 mi |
| 0 | 0.5 | 1 km |

Antsell Rock

PCT

South Peak

San Bernardino National Forest

Red Tahquitz

Hunker Creek

Reeds Meadow

Little Tahquitz Valley

Skunk Cabbage Meadow

PCT

Tahquitz Meadow

PCT

Tahquitz Peak

Saddle Junction

PCT

PCT

SOUTH RIDGE TRAIL

Powderbox Spring

Middle Spring

Jolly Spring

DEVILS SLIDE TRAIL

Lily Rock

Strawberry Creek

Humber Park

FERN VALLEY RD

ERNIE MAXWELL TRAIL

FR 5S11

Suicide Rock

Marion Creek

S CIRCLE DR

TAHQUITZ VIEW DR

PINE AVE

PINE CREST AVE

Idyllwild

243

SAUNDERS MEADOW RD

© The Countryman Press

ELEVATION PROFILE

9,000 ft			Tahquitz Peak	
8,500 ft				
8,000 ft				Saddle Junction
7,500 ft				
7,000 ft	FR 5S11			
6,500 ft	1.0	2.0	3.0	4.0 miles

Hike 32

South Ridge Trail to Saddle Junction

Distance: 10.8 miles round-trip or 7.9 miles via Devil's Slide Trail

Hiking time: 5 hours

Trail highlights: Access to rock climbing, a gateway to other trails, pine forest

Difficulty: ▲▲▲

Family friendly: ▲▲

Scenery: ▲▲

Solitude: ▲

Trail condition: ▲▲▲

GPS TRAILHEAD COORDINATES

UTM Zone	11S
Easting	530373
Northing	3735275
Latitude	N33.75712°
Longitude	W116.67203°

Getting There

From Interstate 215 south of Riverside, exit onto CA 74 east (Exit 15). After entering the San Bernardino National Forest, turn left onto CA 243 toward Idyllwild. Turn right onto Saunders Meadow Road (after Marian View Drive), left onto Pine Avenue, and right onto Tahquitz View Drive. Turn right onto South Ridge Road, and continue to the trailhead on your right.

For a one-way route, park a second car at Humber Park, located at the base of Devil's Slide Trail. To reach Humber Park, take CA 243 north toward Idyllwild. Turn right onto Pine Crest Avenue, right onto South Circle Drive, and take your first left onto Fern Valley Road. Follow Fern Valley Road all the way to Humber Park. You'll need a camping and hiking permit, as well as a National Forest Adventure Pass to park in both areas.

Overview

This straightforward hike on the PCT offers a pleasant there-and-back route by way of South Ridge Trail. The entire hike covers 10.8 miles, though the northbound Pacific Crest Trail portion is 1.4 miles.

Starting from the trailhead, you'll climb 4 miles toward the PCT, passing a spur trail leading to Tahquitz Peak. Once you reach the northbound PCT, the trail is relatively level and shaded. There are several options once you reach Saddle Junction, where a web of trails branches off in various directions. This central hub tends to get crowded with day hikers.

For an overnight option, PCT hikers can continue north toward Wellman Divide for camping in Round Valley. Those wanting a one-way route can head 2.5 miles south on Devil's Slide Trail to Humber Park and then shuttle back to the trailhead for the South Ridge Trail, where the hike begins. Keep in mind that solitude is rare here since Devil's Slide Trail is one of the most popular hikes in the area. It also serves as the gateway to such popular rock climbing spots as Suicide Rock and Lily Rock.

For those who want to experience more of the PCT across this region, Hikes 28 to 34 can be linked together consecutively, allowing for several overnight hikes.

In Detail

Oak and pine decorate the ascent on South Ridge Trail, although some sections might show damage from the 2013 Mountain Fire. The 4-mile trek to the PCT offers great views and a worthwhile half-mile (one-way) spur trail on the right to Tahquitz Peak. At the Tahquitz Peak summit, a fire lookout provides a 360-degree view of the surrounding valleys. Steep switchbacks near the PCT pass oak, chaparral, pine forest, and some impressive boulders.

At the PCT intersection, turn left and continue north, past white granite slopes overlooking Tahquitz Valley to the right. The trail enters a shaded forest before reaching a crossroads clearing called Saddle Junction.

From here, five trails split to Skunk Cabbage Meadow, Tahquitz Valley, Pacific Crest Trails (north and south), and Humber Park (via Devils Slide Trail). This junction also serves as a gateway to Suicide Rock and other popular climbing areas by way of the PCT north to Strawberry Junction. Trails from Saddle Junction get heavy traffic during the fall to summer. To cool off, you might want to extend your trip by hiking from Saddle Junction to Caramba Overlook by way of Reeds Meadow. Here you'll find a swimming hole and waterfall, but this extension will add an additional 4.2 miles (one way) onto your trip from Saddle Junction.

To complete the hike from Saddle Junction, return 5.4 miles to the South Ridge Trail parking area, where you began. For a one

way hike, leave the PCT at Saddle Junction, and head left on Devil's Slide Trail. This will take you 2.5 miles down to Humber Park, but be sure to have a second car parked here so you can shuttle back to South Ridge parking area.

| Gazing into Palm Springs from Caramba Overlook

Park rangers may stop you in this high-trafficked area, so be sure to travel with a Wilderness Visitor Permit, which is available free from the Forest Service Ranger Station (54270 Pine Crest Road, Idyllwild). Permit applications are available at www.fsva.org.

For more information, contact the Idyllwild Ranger Station at 951-659-2117 or 909-382-2921.

Permits are required for day or overnight hikes, and a National Forest Adventure Pass is required to park in this area.

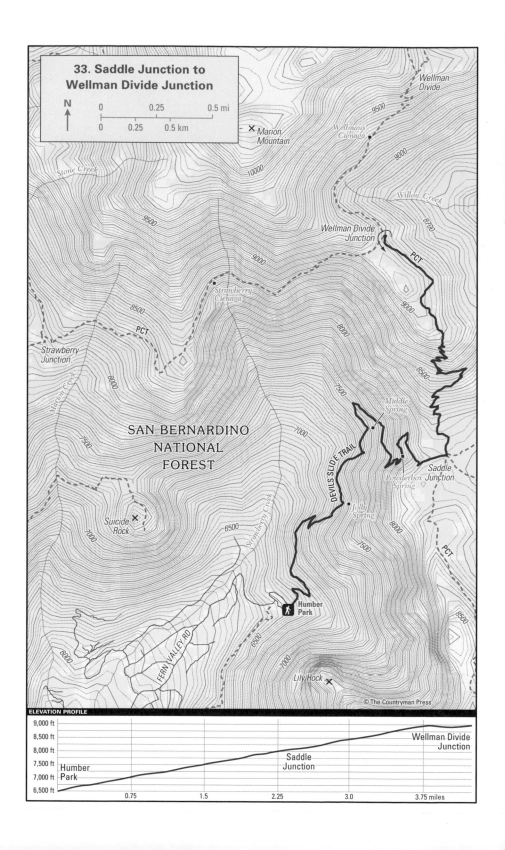

N

| 0 | 0.25 | 0.5 mi |
| 0 | 0.25 | 0.5 km |

Marion
Mountain

Wellman
Divide

9500

Wellmans
Cienaga

9000

Willow Creek

8700

Wellman Divide
Junction

PCT

10000

9500

9000

9000

Strawberry
Cienaga

8500

8000

8500

PCT

Strawberry
Junction

Stone Creek

Marion Creek

8000

7500

7500

Middle
Spring

SAN BERNARDINO
NATIONAL
FOREST

7000

DEVILS SLIDE TRAIL

Powderbox
Spring

Saddle
Junction

Suicide
Rock

7000

6500

Jolly
Spring

8000

7500

PCT

Strawberry Creek

6500

8500

8000

Humber
Park

FERN VALLEY RD.

6500

7000

Lily Rock

© The Countryman Press

ELEVATION PROFILE

9,000 ft					
8,500 ft					
8,000 ft					
7,500 ft					
7,000 ft					
6,500 ft					

Humber
Park

Saddle
Junction

Wellman Divide
Junction

0.75   1.5   2.25   3.0   3.75 miles

Hike 33

Saddle Junction to Wellman Divide Junction

Distance: 8.8 miles round-trip	
Hiking time: 5 hours	
Trail highlights: Sprawling vistas, optional spur trails, surreal rock formations	
Difficulty: ▲ ▲ ▲	
Family friendly: Not recommended	
Scenery: ▲ ▲ ▲	
Solitude: ▲ ▲	
Trail condition: ▲ ▲ ▲	

GPS TRAILHEAD COORDINATES

UTM Zone	11S
Easting	530252
Northing	3737178
Latitude	N33.77429°
Longitude	W116.67327°

Getting There

From Interstate 215 south of Riverside, exit onto CA 74 east (Exit 15). After entering the San Bernardino National Forest, turn left onto CA 243 toward Idyllwild. Turn right onto Pine Crest Avenue and right onto South Circle Drive. Then take your first left onto Fern Valley Road and follow it all the way to Humber Park, located at the trailhead for Devil's Slide Trail.

Arrive early; there is a visitor quota for this trail, which is the main artery into San Jacinto Wilderness. All hikers must obtain Wilderness Visitor Permits from the Forest Service Ranger Station near North Circle Drive on CA 243. A National Forest Adventure Pass is required for parking in this area.

Overview

This trail is the area's most congested due to the foot traffic of Devil's Slide Trail and nearby Wellman Divide, where camping is available in Round Valley. This hike follows Devil's Slide Trail and then goes north along the PCT to the boundary where San Bernardino National Forest meets San Jacinto State Park.

The PCT portion of the hike—covering 2 miles—dramatically follows a steep ridge strewn with massive boulders and towering trees. Views present themselves in nearly every direction and on pristine days extend as far as the Pacific Ocean. Pines and firs grow intermittently between the rocks, although neighboring ridges east of Idyllwild were burned during the 2013 Mountain Fire. After multiple switchbacks, the trail steadily climbs to the picturesque Wellman Divide Junction.

To experience a greater section of the PCT across this region, Hikes 28 to 34 can be linked together consecutively, allowing for several overnight hikes. Camping permits, issued by the U.S. Forest Service, are available up to 90 days in advance from the Idyllwild Ranger Station and can be obtained by calling 951-659-2117 or 909-382-2921. Permit applications are available at www.fsva.org.

In Detail

Be prepared for a workout. The trail gains 2,500 feet in elevation from the start of the hike to the Wellman Junction. From Humber Park, head 2.5 miles northeast, climbing steeply along Devil's Slide Trail.

After 2.5 miles, turn left (north) onto the PCT at Saddle Junction, and follow the signs toward Wellman Divide. The deep sand on the meandering path makes you feel as if you're hiking on the beach. Beyond a trail-border of shrubs and pines, the PCT becomes hard-packed with granite slabs that act as convenient stepping-stones.

The strenuous climb offers views of Suicide Rock to the west. On a clear day, you can see the Pacific Ocean, sadly blanketed by a layer of L.A. smog. You can usually see chalk marks left by climbers who have scaled the rocks of Suicide Rock.

| Suicide Rock

| Approaching Wellman Divide Junction

The trail enters tight switchbacks lined with boulders, white firs, and Jeffrey pines. Spectacular vistas and rock formations make for excellent scenic photography. Continue along the PCT as it climbs and dips, passing two massive, pyramid-shaped rocks. As you near Wellman Divide Junction at 4.4 miles, the trail comes to a three-pronged crossroad; the north heads 1 mile to Wellman Divide, the west continues on the PCT to Strawberry Junction, and the south returns on the PCT to Devil's Slide Trail, where the hike began. This clearing offers shade and smooth rocks for relaxing and enjoying lunch.

For a one-way route, see Hike 34, which begins at Devil's Slide Trail and ends at Deer Springs Trail by way of the PCT and Strawberry Junction. Permit camping is available northeast of Wellman Divide at Tamarack Valley and Round Valley. You're in Mount San Jacinto State Park, which prohibits dogs and fires. To complete the hike, return to the trailhead by way of Devil's Slide Trail.

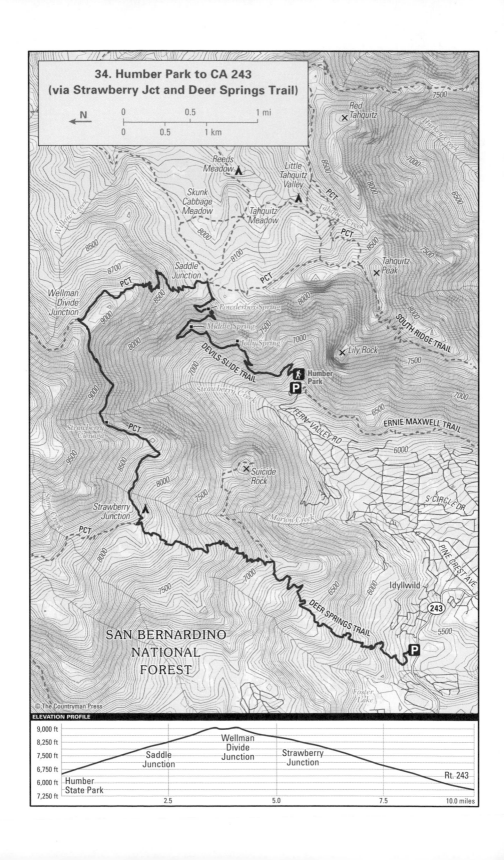

34. Humber Park to CA 243
(via Strawberry Jct and Deer Springs Trail)

N

| 0 | 0.5 | 1 mi |
| 0 | 0.5 | 1 km |

Red Tahquitz

Reeds Meadow

Little Tahquitz Valley

Skunk Cabbage Meadow

Tahquitz Meadow

PCT

Tahquitz Peak

Saddle Junction

PCT

Wellman Divide Junction

PCT

Powderbox Spring

Middle Spring

Jolly Spring

DEVILS SLIDE TRAIL

Lily Rock

SOUTH RIDGE TRAIL

Humber Park

P

Strawberry Creek

FERN VALLEY RD

ERNIE MAXWELL TRAIL

Strawberry Cienaga

PCT

Suicide Rock

S CIRCLE DR

Strawberry Junction

PINE CREST AVE

Marion Creek

Idyllwild

243

PCT

DEER SPRINGS TRAIL

SAN BERNARDINO NATIONAL FOREST

P

© The Countryman Press

Foster Lake

ELEVATION PROFILE

9,000 ft	Wellman Divide Junction	
8,250 ft		
7,500 ft	Saddle Junction	Strawberry Junction
6,750 ft		
6,000 ft	Humber State Park	Rt. 243
7,250 ft		

2.5   5.0   7.5   10.0 miles

Hike 34

Humber Park to CA 243 (via Strawberry Junction and Deer Springs Trail)

Distance: 10.8 miles with shuttle
Hiking time: 5–6 hours
Trail highlights: Mountainside streamlets, forest descent, Strawberry Cienega
Difficulty: ▲ ▲ ▲
Family friendly: ▲ ▲
Scenery: ▲ ▲ ▲
Solitude: ▲
Trail condition: ▲ ▲ ▲

Getting There

From Interstate 215 south of Riverside, exit onto CA 74 east (Exit 15). Turn left onto CA 243 toward Idyllwild. Turn right onto Pine Crest Avenue, right onto South Circle Drive, and left onto Fern Valley Road. Follow Fern Valley Road all the way to Humber Park, located at the base of the Devil's Slide Trail.

Arrive early; there is a visitor quota for this trail, which is the main artery into San Jacinto Wilderness. All hikers must obtain Wilderness Visitor Permits from the Forest Service Ranger Station near North Circle Drive on CA 243. Inside Mount San Jacinto State Park, dogs and fires are not allowed.

This hike description is profiled as a one-way route, which requires shuttling back to Humber Park from the trailhead for the Deer Springs Trail. To park a second car at Deer Springs, head north on CA 243, passing through the town of Idyllwild. The trailhead will be on your right, about 1 mile

past the town. If you've reached Foster Lake or Pine Cove Park, you've gone too far. A National Forest Adventure Pass is required for parking in these areas.

Keep in mind that this hike passes from San Bernardino National Forest into Mount San Jacinto State Park, both of which suffered damage from the 2013 Mountain Fire. These wilderness areas are managed by two agencies and have two separate camping applications. Be sure to obtain the correct application for the location where you will be overnighting.

| Shedding Manzanita branches

For the National Forest, camping permits are available up to 90 days in advance from the Idyllwild Ranger Station and can be obtained by calling 951-659-2117 or 909-382-2921. Permit applications are available at www.fsva.org. For the State Park, permits are available up to 56 days in advance from the San Jacinto State Park office in Idyllwild. Call 951-659-2607 or visit www.parks.ca.gov.

GPS TRAILHEAD COORDINATES	
UTM Zone	11S
Easting	529846
Northing	3738680
Latitude	N33.78785°
Longitude	W116.67761°

Overview

The mountain rivulets of Strawberry Cienega, brilliantly lined with spring wildflowers, add splendor to this picturesque hike. The *cienega* (Spanish for "marsh") offers soft, emerald patches where hikers can rest before a precipitous descent.

This is the reward for tackling the ascending route from Devil's Slide Trail to Wellman Divide Junction (via the PCT). Overnight hikers can camp at Strawberry Junction along the downward gradient. Leaving the Pacific Crest Trail, the hike drops down to CA 243 by way of the arid Deer Springs Trail. From here, hikers can shuttle back along CA 243 to close the "loop" that began at Humber Park and Devil's Slide Trail.

To experience a greater section of the PCT across this region, Hikes 28 to 34 can be linked together consecutively, allowing for several overnight hikes.

| Departing San Jacinto Wilderness

In Detail

Starting at Humber Park, Devil's Slide Trail steeply climbs 2.5 miles northeast to Saddle Junction. There, turn left (north) onto the PCT. Hiking along this forested ridge scattered with boulders and pines will take you to the Wellman Divide Junction in about 2 miles.

Upon reaching this three-way crossroad (Wellman Divide, PCT north and south), head left on this section of the PCT that travels west before bending north again. Continue on the PCT toward Strawberry

splintered trees chewed by tree beetles. A posted sign announces your departure from the San Jacinto Wilderness.

South of the PCT, just before you reach Deer Springs Trail, is the well-maintained Strawberry Junction Camp. You can overnight in this shaded clearing, which has a single outhouse. There is no water here, but you can hike along Deer Springs Trail to nearby Stone Creek, where water trickles from winter through spring. Make sure to purify the water before drinking.

To complete the last portion of the hike, leave the PCT at Strawberry Junction and turn left onto Deer Springs Trail. You will now be entering Mount San Jacinto State Park, where dogs and fires are not permitted. This will descend just over 4 miles into Idyllwild. Threading between white boulders and catclaw shrubs, the route sinks into forest landscape, which is warmer because of the decrease in elevation. The area is filled with gigantic, fairytale-like trees twisted like soft taffy. Stacks of branches neatly border the loose-gravel trail.

Deeper into the descent, the lush landscape fades into desert-like slopes of manzanitas and granite. Switchbacks tighten, periodically overlapping slabs of rock. Purple lupines and scarlet buglers provide occasional patches of color.

About halfway down Deer Springs Trail, a spur trail leads to Suicide Rock, a favorite for climbers. This 1-mile (one-way) detour is worth a side trip if you have the energy.

Closer to CA 243, you'll see thickets of sun-bleached manzanitas. As you cross a sandy wash and pass a forest regulation sign, you can hear the sound of passing cars in the distance. Head toward the power lines near the highway. When you reach the trailhead for the Deer Springs Trail, shuttle back to your starting point at Humber Park, where the hike began at Devil's Slide Trail.

Junction. At the top of the shadeless plateau, white boulders lie beautifully strewn on the hilltop like giant cotton balls.

The trail snakes down the southern shoulder of Marion Mountain, dramatically cutting through slopes of fir and pine. Several switchbacks offer Strawberry Cienega's freshwater rivulets, trickling through spring. This mini oasis gives way to trailside ferns, blue-eyed grass, Indian paintbrush, buttercups, and red monkey flowers.

Splendid mountain views continue until the trail eventually breaks away from the dense forest. It passes a section of

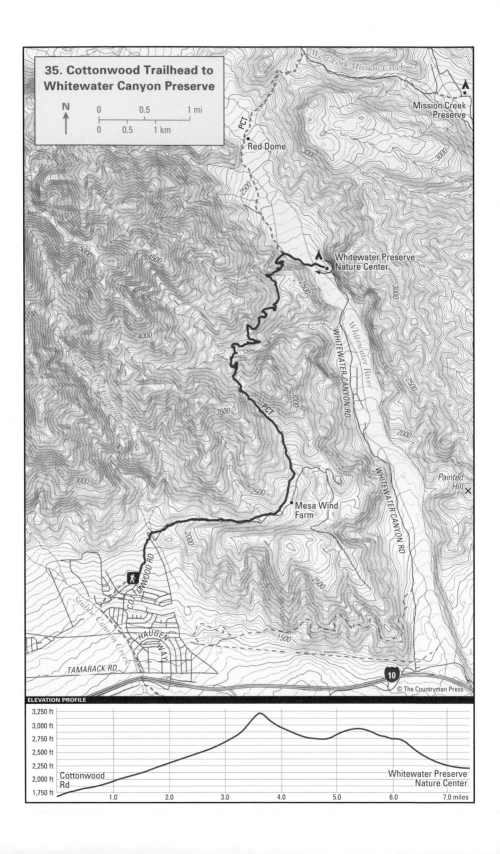

35. Cottonwood Trailhead to Whitewater Canyon Preserve

N

| 0 | 0.5 | 1 mi |
| 0 | 0.5 | 1 km |

West Fork Mission Creek

Mission Creek Preserve

PCT

Red Dome

3000

2500

3000

5000

4500

Whitewater Preserve Nature Center

2500

2500

Whitewater River

4000

WHITEWATER CANYON RD

3000

3500

PCT

3000

2500

2000

Painted Hill

3000

2500

WHITEWATER CANYON RD

Mesa Wind Farm

Cottonwood Canyon

2500

3000

2000

COTTONWOOD RD

Stubbe Canyon Creek

HAUGEN WAY

1500

TAMARACK RD

10

© The Countryman Press

ELEVATION PROFILE

| 3,250 ft |
| 3,000 ft |
| 2,750 ft |
| 2,500 ft |
| 2,250 ft |
| 2,000 ft |
| 1,750 ft |

Cottonwood Rd

Whitewater Preserve Nature Center

1.0   2.0   3.0   4.0   5.0   6.0   7.0 miles

Hike 35

Cottonwood Trailhead to Whitewater Canyon Preserve

Distance: 16 miles round-trip or 8 miles
with shuttle

Hiking time: 4–8 hours

Trail highlights: Flowing river, connected
canyons, abundant wildlife

Difficulty: ▲▲

Family friendly: ▲▲

Scenery: ▲▲▲

Solitude: ▲▲▲▲

Trail condition: ▲▲▲

Getting There

From Los Angeles, take Interstate 10 east,
and exit at Haugen Lehman Way. Turn left
(north) over the freeway, and continue past
Tamarack Road and Sagebrush Avenue to
Cottonwood Drive. Turn right onto Cottonwood Drive, past open fields, power lines,
and small homes. As the pavement fades
into a Jeep trail, look for the PCT post at the
end of Cottonwood Drive. Hikers can either
park at the end of the paved road or continue 0.5 miles north to a dirt parking area,
accessible only to off-road vehicles.

This hike is profiled as a one-way route
from Cottonwood Trailhead to Whitewater Canyon Preserve. To shuttle back from
Whitewater Canyon Preserve, park a second car at 9160 Whitewater Canyon Road,
located northwest of Palm Springs, off Interstate 10. From 10 east, take exit 114 for
Whitewater. Turn left onto Tipton Road and
left onto Whitewater Canyon Road. Continue on Whitewater Canyon Road until it
dead ends at the preserve.

For information about camping in Whitewater Canyon Preserve, call 760-325-7222.
Parking and camping are free, but space is
limited so make a reservation in advance.

GPS TRAILHEAD COORDINATES

UTM Zone	11S
Easting	528188
Northing	3755608
Latitude	N33.94057°
Longitude	W116.69498°

Overview

From windmills and canyons to rivers and
waterfalls, this overnight (or long day) hike
offers numerous surprises. In springtime,
poppies color the hills and in winter, snow
blankets the trail. Against a backdrop of the
seasonally snowcapped mountains of San
Jacinto Peak, a peaceful stream marks the
gateway into San Gorgonio Wilderness.

The PCT drops into Whitewater Canyon, home to endangered birds, mountain
lions, bighorn sheep, and (very rarely seen)
black bears. At the base of this vast canyon is Whitewater Canyon Preserve, where
shaded campsites and manicured gardens
beckon hikers to rest along the river's edge.

| Palm trees backgrounded by snow-capped mountains at Whitewater Canyon Preserve

In Detail

At the end of paved Cottonwood Drive, walk along the Jeep road until it crosses the PCT. Join the northbound PCT, which parallels the road. Cutting through fields of chaparral, the trail climbs toward Mesa Wind Farm, where 4,000 windmills provide enough electricity to power Palm Springs and Coachella Valley.

Continue past a dirt parking area, accessible only to off-road vehicles. After crossing several Jeep roads, the trail passes a streambed where water rarely flows. A cattle gate left of Mesa Wind Park marks the entrance into Gold Canyon. This is also the southern entry point to the PCT's Section C, covering 132.9 miles.

Beyond the gate, the trail crosses Gold Canyon Road twice, now with the windmills directly ahead. At the second crossing, the PCT climbs west of the road and continues toward the Mesa Wind Park office. A sign points hikers toward shade and water, compliments of Mesa Wind Park management. (Keep in mind that water is available only during operating hours, 6 A.M. to noon, Monday through Friday.)

Yucca, creosote, cacti, and rabbitbrush line the trail, brightened in spring by yellow brittlebush, a plant once used as incense in California's first churches. After briefly joining a dirt road, the PCT narrows once again. With the sound of windmill blades chopping at the sky, the steady climb out of Gold Canyon begins. Be sure to check weather conditions prior to the trek, as this section is often icy in winter and can reach 100-plus degrees in summer.

The steepest section of the hike takes place near 3 miles. Having gained more than 1,000 feet in elevation, the trail crosses a wash toward the canyon's west shoulder. Three switchbacks lead to the canyon ridge and its stunning north- and south-facing views.

At 2,800 feet, a welcome descent begins. Follow the pleasant pass down several switchbacks that lead to Teutang Canyon. Entering San Gorgonio Wilderness, the PCT crosses North Fork Mission Creek. Traverse along the canyon shoulder, noting the trees that line the canyon to the right. The trail enters a chaparral area often populated by quail and lizards. Gradually descend into the canyon, following the tight switchbacks that lead to Whitewater River, which flows year-round.

As you reach the canyon floor, pass through a metal gate and head right (south), away from the PCT. Follow the yellow trail signs to Whitewater Canyon Preserve, 2,851 acres that include the former Whitewater Trout Farm. In 2006, Friends of the Desert Mountains and the Coachella Valley Mountains Conservancy purchased the 291-acre farm. A half-mile from the PCT, it now serves as a visitors center. Drinking water, restrooms, and 60 campsites are available free of charge.

To reach the east bank of the river, continue on the marked trail, over wooden-plank crossings. This canyon oasis provides a safe haven for the endangered southwest willow flycatcher and Bell's vireo. Hikers may also come across bear and deer tracks, although this is quite rare. Towering above the picnic area and fish ponds are vertical cliffs where bighorn sheep thrive. Mountain lions and rattlesnakes also live in this area.

To reach this point of the hike, parallel the east side of the river toward the visitors center. For a one way route, shuttle from here back to the Cottonwood trailhead, where the hike began. If time permits, overnight at Whitewater Canyon Preserve and hike back (rather than shuttle) to the Cottonwood trailhead the following day. This there-and-back option would make this a 16-mile round-trip hike, rather than an 8-mile shuttle hike. Embark on the journey early in the morning, especially during summer months when the scorching sun beats down on the trail.

| Climbing toward Mesa Wind Farm

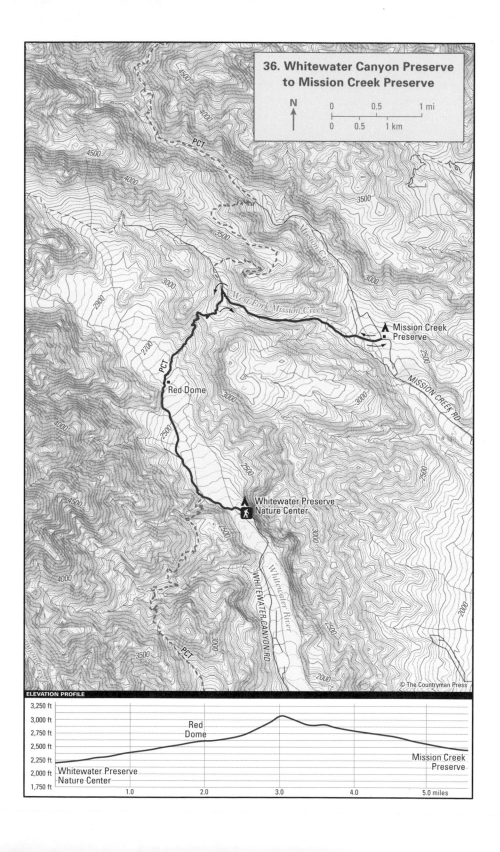

36. Whitewater Canyon Preserve
to Mission Creek Preserve

N

| 0 | 0.5 | 1 mi |
| 0 | 0.5 | 1 km |

PCT

4500

4000

4500

4000

3500

Mission Creek

3500

3000

3000

West Fork Mission Creek

Mission Creek
Preserve

PCT

2100

2200

Red Dome

3000

2500

2500

3000

2500

MISSION CREEK RD

2500

4500

2500

Whitewater Preserve
Nature Center

2500

3000

4000

3000

WHITEWATER CANYON RD

Whitewater River

2500

PCT

3500

2000

2000

© The Countryman Press

ELEVATION PROFILE

3,250 ft				
3,000 ft			Red	
2,750 ft			Dome	
2,500 ft				
2,250 ft				Mission Creek
2,000 ft	Whitewater Preserve			Preserve
1,750 ft	Nature Center			

1.0   2.0   3.0   4.0   5.0 miles

Hike 36

Whitewater Canyon Preserve to Mission Creek Preserve

Distance. 14 miles round-trip or 7 miles
with shuttle

Hiking time: 4–7 hours

Trail highlights: Perennial river, canyon
traverse, seasonal wildflowers

Difficulty: ▲ ▲ ▲

Family friendly: ▲

Scenery: ▲ ▲ ▲

Solitude: ▲ ▲ ▲

Trail condition: ▲ ▲ ▲

Getting There

Heading east on Interstate 10 from Los Angeles, take the 114/Waterwater exit. Turn left onto Tipton Road and left onto Whitewater Canyon Road. Continue 4.5 miles until you reach Whitewater Canyon Preserve, at the end of the paved road. Park in the designated area beside the Whitewater Ranger Station. The trailhead begins just north of the fishing pond, beyond two large palm trees.

For a one-way hike, park a second car at Mission Creek Preserve and shuttle 15 miles back to Whitewater Canyon Preserve, where the hike will begin. To get to Mission Creek Preserve, take I-10 to Highway 62 (Twentynine Palms Highway). Then take Highway 62 toward Yucca Valley, and continue 5 miles toward Mission Creek Road. Turn left (west) and drive 2.25 miles until you reach a locked gate, accessible only by combination provided by the desert field

office. Free parking and camping are available beside the Mission Creek stone house at the end of the dirt road. It is best to reserve space one week in advance. For information regarding access to Mission Creek Preserve, call the desert field office at 760-369-7105.

Free camping and parking is also available at Whitewater Canyon Preserve. For trail conditions and reservations, call the Whitewater Canyon Preserve office at 760-325-7222.

GPS TRAILHEAD COORDINATES

UTM Zone	11S
Easting	531731
Northing	3761048
Latitude	N33.98953°
Longitude	W116.65644°

Overview

The Whitewater Canyon and Mission Creek Preserves are part of the Wildlands Conservancy's 33,000-acre Sand-to-Snow Preserve System. Launching from Whitewater Canyon Preserve, the hike traverses the banks of the Whitewater River, flowing from the San Gorgonio Mountains. Riparian vegetation, grasslands, and low-lying forest offer refuge to mountain lions, bighorn sheep, black bears, and endangered birds.

Joining the PCT, the route skirts Red Dome and zigzags toward the Whitewater

| Mountain lion footprint

In Detail

To start, head north from the Whitewater Ranger Station, and follow the stone-lined trail to the first river crossing. The trail passes over several rivulets before curving north and heading directly through the canyon.

Follow the rock-strewn trail, past the low-forested lands of sycamores, cottonwoods, willows, and shrubs. After half a mile, the trail merges north (right) with the PCT. Still heading upstream parallel to the river, the route requires a considerable amount of rock-hopping to stay on track.

After crossing a wash, enter the center of the narrow canyon, winding past clusters of beavertail cactus, yucca, and brittle bushes. The trail enters a wide-open section peppered with gray boulders. Although somewhat difficult to follow, the PCT is periodically marked by posts surrounded by piles of stones.

Around 1.5 miles, the trail crosses the river a final time, passing over logs that serve as a makeshift bridge. As the river veers left, the PCT steadily climbs out of the canyon. Switchbacks soon take you to the saddle at 3,000 feet, where views embrace San Jacinto Peak, San Gorgonio Peak, and Whitewater Canyon. A rewarding descent begins beyond the ridge. At the time of this writing, this part of the trail was slightly overgrown with catclaws and foxtails.

After passing the volcanic mound to the right known as "Red Dome," continue approximately 1 mile to West Fork Mission Creek. This area can get rather complicated due to Jeep roads and gullies that blend with the trail. Once you reach the base of the canyon, break away from the PCT and head east rather than climbing north out of the canyon. Continue 2 miles toward North Fork Mission Creek, named for the Serrano Tribe of Mission Indians that populated the San Bernardino Mountains until 1834.

Canyon ridge. Distant views of Mount San Jacinto fade as the PCT drops to the other side of the canyon, slowly descending and continuing toward a link to Mission Creek Preserve, where hikers can overnight or shuttle back to Whitewater Canyon Preserve.

If time allows, camp at Mission Creek Preserve, and then explore farther north on the PCT the following day. Eventually The PCT heads to Big Bear and beyond (see Hike #37). Adding a few miles north on the PCT is a pleasant way to enjoy the area before returning south to Whitewater Canyon Preserve, where the hike begins.

Don't forget to bring binoculars. As a gateway between the San Berardino and San Jacinto Mountains, the preserves are home to a variety of wildlife, including the endangered Bell's vireo and the southwest willow flycatcher. Begin your hike in the early morning to maximize your chances of seeing myriad creatures—particularly the bighorn sheep that clamber along the cliffs. Winter hikers may encounter patches of snow, although low elevations and open lands tend to keep this region fairly warm year-round. River crossings can be dangerous after heavy rains. For trail conditions, call the Whitewater Canyon Preserve office at 760-325-7222.

| Whitewater River

Follow the trail markers to the historic Stone House and picnic area, open to the public as part of the Mission Creek Preserve. Camping facilities are available free of charge, but reservations must be made one week in advance due to limited space and a gate combination to access the area. From here, hikers can either shuttle back to Whitewater Canyon Preserve or overnight at Mission Creek and explore farther north along the PCT the following day.

To do the latter, return to the PCT from Mission Creek Preserve, and veer north. The trail switches back and climbs out of the second canyon. Upon reaching the ridge, the PCT doubles back, giving a clear view of the snaking trail just conquered.

Once out of the canyon, the landscape dramatically changes to a plateau of manzanitas and pale stones. Continue north while absorbing distant views of rippling valleys.

A good point to turn around is just beyond this chaparral ridge, having now reached 3,600 feet in elevation. Head back in the direction from which you came, hiking south on the PCT. You won't need to take the spur trail to Mission Creek Preserve on your return trip unless you plan to camp another night. Keep in mind that the canyons are fully shaded by 3 P.M. in winter.

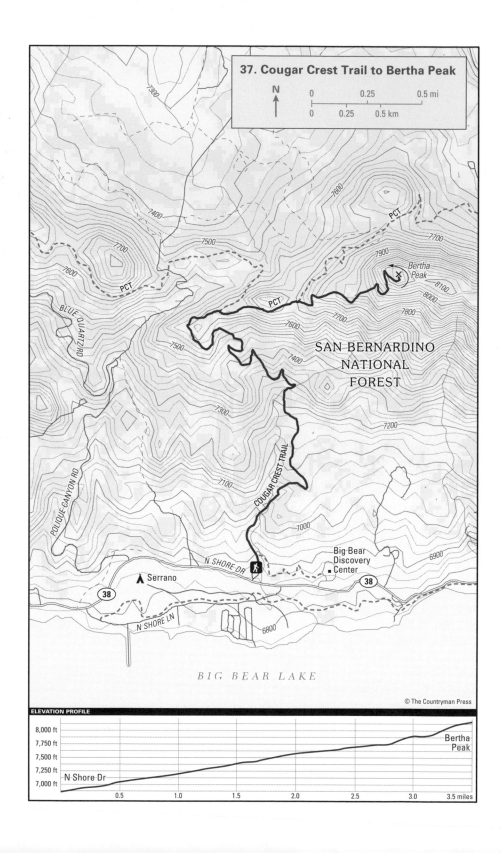

37. Cougar Crest Trail to Bertha Peak

N

| 0 | 0.25 | 0.5 mi |
| 0 | 0.25 | 0.5 km |

7300

7600

PCT

7400

7500

7700

7600

PCT

BLUE QUARTZ RD

7900

Bertha Peak

7700

8100

8000

7800

PCT

7600

7700

SAN BERNARDINO NATIONAL FOREST

7500

7400

7200

7300

POLIQUE CANYON RD

7100

COUGAR CREST TRAIL

7000

6900

N SHORE DR

Big Bear Discovery Center

Serrano

38

38

N SHORE LN

6800

© The Countryman Press

BIG BEAR LAKE

ELEVATION PROFILE

8,000 ft
7,750 ft
7,500 ft
7,250 ft
7,000 ft

Bertha Peak

N Shore Dr

0.5   1.0   1.5   2.0   2.5   3.0   3.5 miles

Hike 37

Cougar Crest Trail to Bertha Peak

Distance: 6.5 miles round-trip

Hiking time: 3 hours

Trail highlights: Views of Big Bear Lake, snowcapped mountains, piñon pines and junipers

Difficulty: ▲ ▲ ▲

Family friendly: ▲ ▲

Scenery: ▲ ▲ ▲ ▲

Solitude: ▲ ▲

Trail condition: ▲ ▲ ▲

Getting There

From Big Bear City, take Highway 18 west. Turn right at Stanfield Cutoff, which crosses over Big Bear Lake and intersects Highway 38. Turn left at Highway 38 and follow the northern shore of the lake for 1.3 miles. Just past the Big Bear Discovery Center, turn right into the Cougar Crest paved parking area.

From Fawnskin, head east 2.4 miles on Highway 38. The Cougar Crest parking area will be on the left side of the highway.

With space for approximately 50 cars, this area can get crowded when families head to the hills for a day of sledding in winter. Parked vehicles must display a Forest Service Adventure Pass, available for $5 per day from the Discovery Center, 0.6 miles from the trailhead for the Cougar Crest Trail.

Note: Goldsmith's Board House in Big Bear rents snowshoes for winter hiking. Visit www.goldsmithsboardandski.com or call 909-866-2728.

GPS TRAILHEAD COORDINATES

UTM Zone	11S
Easting	508214
Northing	3791479
Latitude	N34.26442°
Longitude	W116.91078°

Overview

What begins as a gradual ascent up Cougar Crest Trail soon becomes a challenging climb that is sure to leave hikers breathless at times. With a 1,500-foot elevation gain and what seem to be an endless number of switchbacks, every step toward Bertha Peak becomes more demanding than the one before. Fortunately, efforts are rewarded at the 8,201-foot summit, where views span from Holcomb Valley to Big Bear Lake. April through November typically presents ideal weather conditions for this hike. However, with snowshoes and proper attire and hiking gear, the route beckons during winter months as well. Large radio towers at the top of Bertha Peak serve as a constant destination marker, even when snow covers the trail.

In Detail

Although the highlight of this hike is the panorama from Bertha Peak, the view during the 2-mile climb along Cougar Crest

| Winter hike on Cougar Crest Trail

Trail to the PCT is equally enthralling. From the parking area, follow the well-maintained path through a fragrant forest of juniper and Jeffrey Pines. Just beyond the Cougar Crest Trail trailhead is a wooden bridge leading 0.6 miles to the Big Bear Discovery Center. Pass this spur and continue along the gradually ascending Cougar Crest Trail, which once served as a fire road. The route becomes increasingly steep after the first mile. Piñon pines populate the surrounding, densely forested area and are notable in their wild twists upward from buried roots.

Several switchbacks lead to pleasant views of Big Bear Lake. Follow the winding route, past a paralleling ravine until you reach the Cougar Crest–PCT junction. Keep in mind that this initial section, a favorite for runners, bikers, and families, tends to be more crowded than the challenging climb up to Bertha Peak.

Having just completed 2 miles, turn right at the junction and continue along the PCT. Stay on the trail until it crosses a dirt road leading to Bertha Peak, about half a mile from the junction. Take that road for a half-mile, toward the easily identifiable radio antennas.

Shade from mountain mahogany, Western junipers, and piñon pines relieves some of the effort of the climb as the trail switches back several times before finally reaching the base of the radio towers. Making it well worth the journey are 360-degree views of Big Bear Lake, Delamar Mountain, Holcomb Valley, the San Gorgonio Wilderness, and the Mojave Desert.

Considering the 8,201-foot elevation, this hike is still moderate and can be accomplished in a single afternoon. After absorbing the spectacular vistas, return to the trailhead for the Cougar Crest Trail by going in the direction from which you came.

Those who intend to camp in this area can overnight at Serrano Campground on the north shore of Big Bear Lake. Food supplies are available in the town of Fawnskin to the west or in Big Bear City to the east.

Hike 38

Polique Canyon Road to Delamar Mountain

Distance: 5 miles round-trip

Hiking time: 3 hours

Trail highlights: Views of Big Bear Lake, snowcapped mountains, forest trail

Difficulty: ▲▲

Family friendly: ▲▲▲

Scenery: ▲▲▲

Solitude: ▲▲▲

Trail condition: ▲▲▲

For winter hikes, Goldsmith's Board House in Big Bear rents snowshoes. Visit www.goldsmithsboardandski.com or call 909-866-2728.

GPS TRAILHEAD COORDINATES	
UTM Zone	11S
Easting	507624
Northing	3793614
Latitude	N34.28369°
Longitude	W116.91717°

Getting There

From San Bernardino, head northeast to the junction with SR 330. Just beyond Running Springs, take the SR 18 all the way to the Big Bear Lake Dam. At the dam, turn left onto SR 38 (North Shore Drive) toward Fawnskin. Turn left at mile marker 54.4 onto Polique Canyon Road. Continue 2 miles uphill to the sign for Holcomb View Trail.

From the town of Big Bear, take the Stanfield Cutoff across the lake to the intersection of Stanfield and North Shore Drive (SR 38). Head west (left), past the Discovery Center, all the way to Polique Canyon Road. Turn right and follow the road 2 miles uphill until you reach the sign for Holcomb View Trail and the PCT.

Park on the side of the road, and be sure to display a Forest Adventure Pass when parking in this area. The hike begins on the west (left) side of Polique Canyon Road.

Overview

Delamar Mountain, on the northwest end town, was named for a local miner who once worked in this area. It offers views of Fawnskin, Big Bear Lake, and the San Bernardino Mountains. Although the PCT leading to Delamar's base is clearly marked, plan for an adventure to reach the summit. In fact, the boulder-strewn mountain is void of a designated trail, despite it being a prominent peak at 8,400 feet. While most people trek the route in spring and summer, it is equally stunning in late winter, when snow decorates the branches of towering pines.

In Detail

From Polique Canyon Road, begin on the PCT heading northwest (left), opposite of the Holcomb View Trail sign. At the time of writing, the PCT post was missing on the

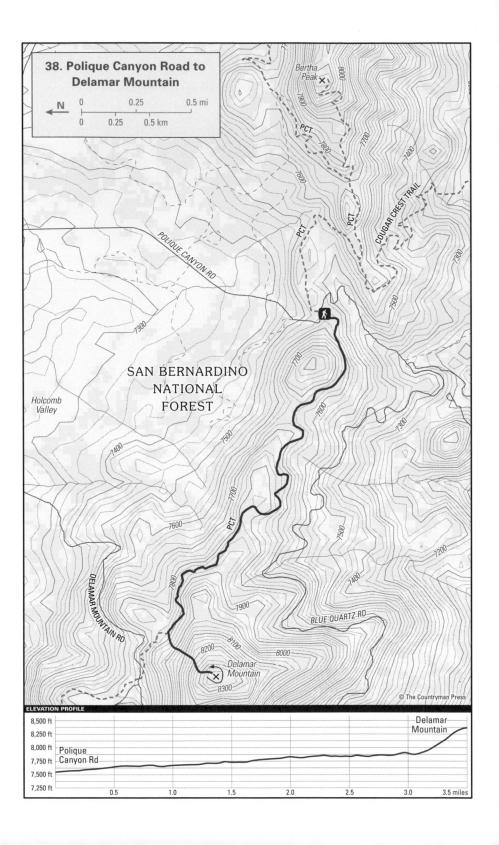

38. Polique Canyon Road to Delamar Mountain

N

| 0 | 0.25 | 0.5 mi |
| 0 | 0.25 | 0.5 km |

Bertha Peak ✕

8000

7900

7800

7700

PCT

7600

PCT

PCT

COUGAR CREST TRAIL

7500

7400

7300

POLIQUE CANYON RD

7300

SAN BERNARDINO NATIONAL FOREST

Holcomb Valley

7700

7600

7500

7400

7600

PCT

7700

7500

7400

7200

7300

DELAMAR MOUNTAIN RD

7800

7900

BLUE QUARTZ RD

8100

8200

8000

Delamar Mountain ✕

8300

© The Countryman Press

ELEVATION PROFILE

8,500 ft							Delamar
8,250 ft							Mountain
8,000 ft	Polique						
7,750 ft	Canyon Rd						
7,500 ft							
7,250 ft							
	0.5	1.0	1.5	2.0	2.5	3.0	3.5 miles

| Big Bear Lake

west side of the road. From the initial steps, hikers are treated to mountain and lake views, which periodically disappear behind black oaks and Jeffrey pines. Half a mile into the hike, the PCT enters an open clearing before narrowing back onto the forest trail. Traverse along the ridge for just over a mile, with the lake to your left.

Just beyond the first mile, the trail curves north (right), leaving behind any glimpse of the lake. To the left are distant views of Delamar Mountain, which you will eventually ascend. The PCT curves right and then left, now providing a new landscape of Holcomb Valley to the north. Named for William F. Holcomb, the valley gained fame after the miner struck gold in 1860, thus launching the largest gold rush in Southern California history.

In winter, this portion of the PCT has nearly twice as much snow as the section where the hike commenced, due to the dense forest that blocks the sun. This shaded area can also get quite windy, so be sure to pack a windbreaker.

Around 2.2 miles, pass a ravine to your right, and leave the PCT for Delamar Mountain to your immediate left. This spot is somewhat difficult to pinpoint, especially since there are only ribbons of undefined trails heading northwest to the summit. Select the most direct and passable route, about 0.2 mile to the top. The climb is steep, but rewarding and relatively brief. The more level summit is usually marked by a cairn. From here, you can see Holcomb Valley to the north and Big Bear Lake to the south.

To complete the hike, return in the direction from which you came, down Delamar Mountain, south on the PCT, and back to the trailhead at Polique Canyon Road. From March through November, overnight camping is available at nearby Serrano Campground, located at 40650 North Shore Lane. For reservations, call 909-866-8550.

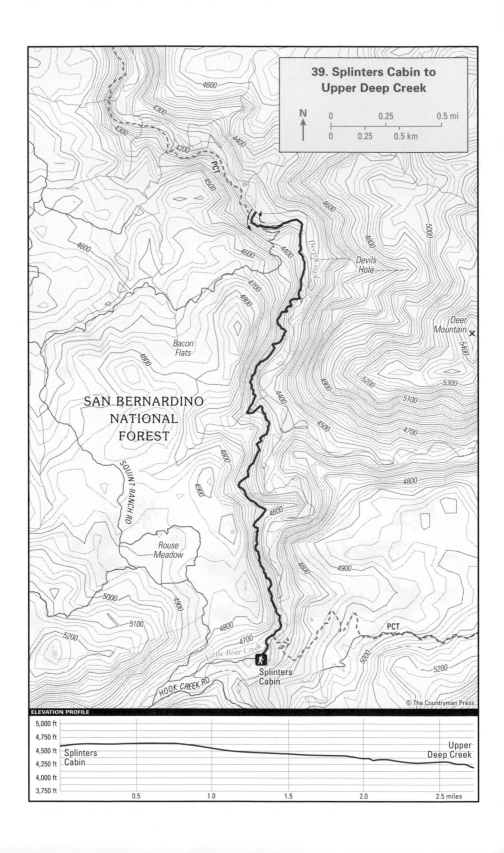

39. Splinters Cabin to
Upper Deep Creek

N
0   0.25   0.5 mi
0   0.25   0.5 km

4600
4300
4200
PCT
4500
4400
Devils Creek
Devils
Hole
4600
4800
5000
4600
4700
4800
4800
Deer
Mountain ✕
5400
Bacon
Flats
4800
SAN BERNARDINO
NATIONAL
FOREST
4400
4500
4900
5200
5100
5300
4700
4800
SQUINT RANCH RD
4800
4900
4600
4800
4900
Rouse
Meadow
5000
4900
4800
PCT
5000
4600
5100
5200
4700
Cattle Bear Creek
5000
5200
HOOK CREEK RD
Splinters
Cabin

© The Countryman Press

ELEVATION PROFILE

	0.5	1.0	1.5	2.0	2.5 miles
5,000 ft					
4,750 ft					
4,500 ft	Splinters				Upper
4,250 ft	Cabin				Deep Creek
4,000 ft					
3,750 ft					

Hike 39

Splinters Cabin to Upper Deep Creek

Distance: 6 miles round-trip

Hiking time: 3 hours

Trail highlights: Rushing Deep Creek, dramatic canyon, swimming hole

Difficulty: ▲▲

Family friendly: ▲▲▲

Scenery: ▲▲▲▲

Solitude: ▲▲▲

Trail condition: ▲▲▲

Getting There

From Highway 18 and the 173 junction, head north on the 173 toward Lake Arrowhead. Head east (right) on Highway 173 toward the community of Cedar Glen. Turn right onto Hook Creek Road, which becomes Forest Road (2N26Y). Veer left at the junction with 3N34 and right at the junction with 3N34C. Continue half a mile on the dirt road to Splinters Cabin trailhead. After rains, this pitted road can get extremely muddy, so

| Deep Creek at Splinters Cabin trailhead

drive with caution. A Forest Adventure Pass is required to park in the area. This marks the starting point for the hike along the PCT to Upper Deep Creek.

GPS TRAILHEAD COORDINATES	
UTM Zone	11S
Easting	488135
Northing	3792416
Latitude	N34.27284°
Longitude	W117.12890°

Overview

This wild creek, flowing north from the San Bernardino Mountains, is one of the highlights of Southern California's PCT. It savagely cascades through gaping canyons past jagged boulders, with a brief interlude at a swimming hole where nomads gather to bathe in the placid pool. Commencing at Splinters Cabin, this portion of the PCT is where you'll get your solitude-fix since most hikers who wish to take a dip visit the Deep Creek Hot Springs farther north. Plan to see a plethora of diverse flora, ranging from sycamores and cottonwoods to yucca and chaparral at lower elevations. The main draw, however, is the relentless view of Deep Creek, a state-designated Wild Trout Stream popular with anglers. This hike can be enjoyed year-round but is best October through May.

In Detail

Begin at the Splinters Cabin trailhead, named after the fishing cabin built by Le Roy Raymond in 1922. (His wife said it was full of splinters, hence the name.) Stay to the left of Deep Creek, crossing over a tributary before working your way to the top of the bridge by following the slope. Do not go over the bridge since this will lead you away from the PCT. On the northbound route, the river should always remain to your right.

Climbing steadily, the PCT leaves the banks of the creek and stays high on an oak-lined ridge that skirts the canyon. Pay close attention to your footing since sections of the trail are narrow and give way to near-vertical drops to the right. As the creek widens and calms briefly, the trail bends left to a side channel of water spilling in from Holcomb Creek. Cross over the rivulet, and follow the PCT as it switches back right toward Deep Creek.

After 1.5 miles, pass boulder walls and steep drops, backed by visions of Deer Mountain to the north. After a left bend, the creek and the PCT curve in unison, both snaking in tandem at varying elevations. Notice the sandy shore at the base of the canyon, reminiscent of a private beach on the water's edge.

Departing from greener vegetation of sycamores, willows, and cottonwoods, at 2.5 miles the trail nears Bacon Flats, where cactus, Our Lord's Candle, and chaparral are abundant. To the north is Devil's Hole, which lies just beyond Deer Mountain. Approaching 3 miles, the PCT intersects Forest Road 3N34D. Leave the PCT and turn right, following the dirt road to the banks of Upper Deep Creek. This swimming hole lures hikers when temperatures rise but is relatively empty in winter.

The turnaround point, this area is home to golden eagles, mountain lions, deer, squirrels, owls, and the endangered arroyo toad. Be sure to check your pack and yourself for ticks, since this part of the trail is infested with them, especially between April and November. From here, return in the direction from which you came, back to the Splinters Cabin parking area.

| Cliff view of Upper Deep Creek

| Historic Cajon Pass |

PART IV

San Gabriel Mountains
and Angeles National Forest

| Towering agave stalk |

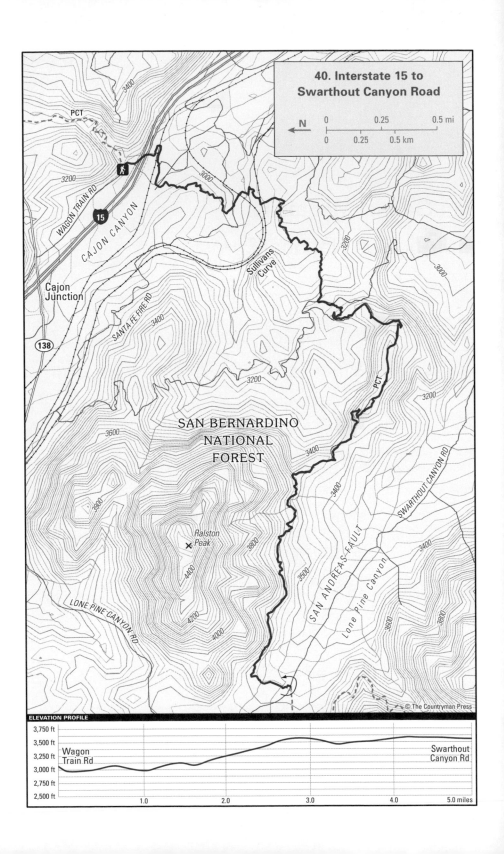

40. Interstate 15 to Swarthout Canyon Road

N

| 0 | 0.25 | 0.5 mi |
| 0 | 0.25 | 0.5 km |

PCT

WAGON TRAIN RD

15

CAJON CANYON

Cajon
Junction

138

SANTA FE FIRE RD

Sullivans
Curve

3400
3200
3000
3200
3200
3000
3400
3400

PCT

SWARTHOUT CANYON RD

SAN BERNARDINO
NATIONAL
FOREST

3600
3200
3400
3900
3800
Ralston
× Peak
4400
4200
4000
3500
3600
3800
3600
3400

LONE PINE CANYON RD

SAN ANDREAS FAULT

Lone Pine Canyon

© The Countryman Press

ELEVATION PROFILE

3,750 ft					
3,500 ft					
3,250 ft	Wagon				Swarthout
3,000 ft	Train Rd				Canyon Rd
2,750 ft					
2,500 ft	1.0	2.0	3.0	4.0	5.0 miles

Hike 40

Interstate 15 to Swarthout Canyon Road

Distance: 10.28 miles round-trip

Hiking time: 4–5 hours

Trail highlights: Views of Ralston Peak
and Mormon Rocks

Difficulty: ▲▲

Family friendly: ▲

Scenery: ▲▲

Solitude: ▲▲

Trail condition: ▲▲▲

Getting There

From Interstate 15 north, take the Palmdale Highway 138/Silverwood Lake exit south of Cajon Junction. From the off-ramp, head east on Highway 138, and take the first right onto Wagon Train Road. Now paralleling Interstate 15, this frontage road continues 0.6 miles south to the PCT. Just before the trailhead are a mini market, restaurant, and gas station, where hikers can stock up on supplies. Street parking is available near the

| Soaking in the Mormon Rocks view

PCT trailhead at a stone monument dedicated to the Santa Fe Trail Pioneers.

Clearly visible, the trail is located on the left side of the dead-end road, across the highway from a truck-weighing station. Cars parked in this area must display a National Forest Adventure Pass.

GPS TRAILHEAD COORDINATES

UTM Zone	11S
Easting	457110
Northing	3796190
Latitude	N34.30606°
Longitude	W117.46612°

Overview

Contrasting with the concrete landscape of Interstate 15, the trail guides hikers from a daunting freeway tunnel into creek-and-canyon country framed by wild oaks. A brief jaunt through desert chaparral leads to Sullivan's Curve and its historic Cajon Pass, often trafficked by trains and photographed by rail fans.

The Mormon Rocks, also known as the Rock Candy Mountains, create a memorable backdrop. Highlighting the journey near the turnaround point is the striking traverse across a high ridge, with Ralston Peak to the east and Lone Pine Canyon to the west. Just beyond 5 miles, the trail spills onto Swarthout Canyon Road, marking the turnaround point for a there-and-back trek.

The San Gabriel Mountains portion of the PCT stretches 170 miles north from Cajon Pass to Liebre Mountain and creates the divide between Los Angeles County and the Mojave Desert. This trail, on the southernmost section of the San Gabriels, affords a glimpse of the beauty that lies ahead.

Although this section of the PCT does not reach such extreme elevations, other portions can climb above 9,000 feet, leaving mountain ranges blanketed with snow through June. While you should be sure to check weather conditions before hiking, this manageable trail will eventually conclude at 3,556 feet.

In Detail

To begin this 10.28-mile hike, start from Wagon Train Road. Pass the white metal gate, and enter the clearly marked PCT via the tunnel under Interstate 15. You'll emerge onto a beach-like path beside a peaceful stream where water flows year-round. It makes this riparian area a breeding ground for the endangered arroyo southwestern toad. In summer, birds such as the southwestern willow flycatcher and the yellow warbler migrate to this sheltered zone.

Logs scattered in the streambed make for a safe crossing. From here, pass under a wooden trestle that supports this segment of the historic Santa Fe Railway. Built in the early 1880s, it served as the first railroad route to use Cajon Pass, a link between the mountains of San Bernardino and San Gabriel. Reaching 4,000 feet, Cajon Pass itself is often besieged by high winds, wildfires, and the occasional snowstorm. Check trail conditions prior to hiking, and be sure to pack a windbreaker.

Beyond the trestle, the PCT bends to the right, paralleling a farmhouse to the left. Entering a desert chaparral landscape, hikers cross a Jeep road before ascending a sandy ridge. Through spring, purple Mecca-aster, scarlet bugler, yellow brittlebrush, and other colorful wildflowers remain in bloom. Stunning red toyon shrubs, commonly known as Christmas berries, add color to the hills year-round.

Continue on the PCT past a small cave around 1 mile that could serve as emer-

| Christmas berries add color to the hills year-round.

gency shelter. After dipping into a wash, cross over a dirt road that leads into a metal culvert. With the train tracks now to the right, the trail offers stunning views of the distant Mormon Rocks, named for Mormon settlers who made their way from Salt Lake City to Los Angeles in the 1850s. Looking like its nickname, the Rock Candy Mountains, the massif has taken its bizarre formation from centuries of harsh weather.

After crossing the railroad tracks, follow the trail to the right, pausing briefly at the boulder platform at 1.5 miles. This is an excellent spot for soaking in the beauty of the majestic Mormon Rocks. Just past this point, the PCT turns left onto a dirt road and continues 100 yards until it narrows and drops to the right. Soon the route parallels

a creek bed on the left, where golden sycamores glisten until early December.

Just beyond 2 miles, the trail passes two power-line roads, the second climbing to the left. Narrowing once again, the PCT curves to the right along a steep ridge that approaches the San Andreas Fault. This traverse cuts between the south face of Ralston Peak and the north side of Lone Pine Canyon.

After several switchbacks and crossing a wash, the trail enters a field of century plants and passes a cache where drinking water is usually available. Follow the PCT to the left until it meets Swarthout Canyon Road. At 5.14 miles, you'll reach the turnaround point for the hike. To complete the journey, return to the trailhead at Wagon Train Road.

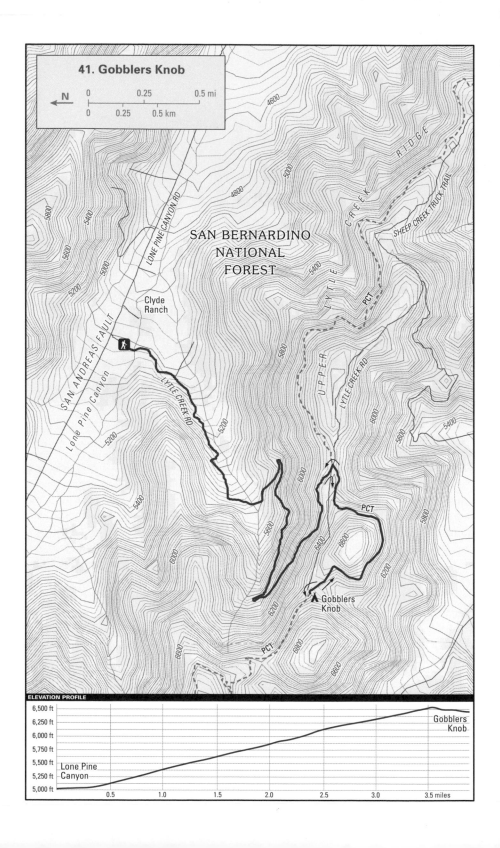

41. Gobblers Knob

N

| 0 | 0.25 | 0.5 mi |

| 0 | 0.25 | 0.5 km |

4600

5800

5400

5600

5000

5200

LONE PINE CANYON RD.

4800

5000

SAN BERNARDINO
NATIONAL
FOREST

Clyde
Ranch

SAN ANDREAS FAULT

Lone Pine Canyon

5200

5400

5200

LYTLE CREEK RD.

5600

6000

5400

5800

UPPER

LYTLE

CREEK

RIDGE

SHEEP CREEK TRUCK TRAIL

PCT

LYTLE CREEK RD.

6000

5600

5400

5800

5800

6200

6000

6400

6600

PCT

6200

6200

Gobblers
Knob

6600

PCT

6600

6800

ELEVATION PROFILE

6,500 ft								Gobblers
6,250 ft								Knob
6,000 ft								
5,750 ft								
5,500 ft								
5,250 ft	Lone Pine							
5,000 ft	Canyon							
	0.5	1.0	1.5	2.0	2.5	3.0	3.5 miles	

Hike 41

Gobblers Knob

Distance: 7 miles round-trip	
Hiking time: 3 hours	
Trail highlights: Upper Lytle Creek Divide, snowcapped mountains	
Difficulty: ▲▲▲	
Family friendly: ▲	
Scenery: ▲▲	
Solitude: ▲▲	
Trail condition: ▲▲▲	

GPS TRAILHEAD COORDINATES

UTM Zone	11S
Easting	447585
Northing	3798370
Latitude	N34.32528°
Longitude	W117.56976°

Getting There

From Interstate 15, take SR 138 west. Continue 1.25 miles until you reach Lone Pine Canyon Road. Turn left and follow the route 5.4 miles to Lytle Creek Road (3N31). Park at the base of the dirt road at the entrance to Clyde Ranch, which is usually locked and covered with snow in winter. For the winter hike described here, park at the bottom of Lytle Creek Road, where it meets Lone Pine Canyon Road. Don your snowshoes to walk 3 miles along snowbound Lytle Creek Road to the PCT trailhead.

Otherwise, for a short hike to Gobblers Knob (when the route is clear of snow), you can drive up Lytle Creek Road beyond the ridgeline to its PCT intersection, where parking is available. At any time, in either parking area, all vehicles must display a Forest Adventure Pass, available for $5 per day at gas stations and grocery stores in the area.

Overview

Ascending the northern section of Upper Lytle Creek Divide, the hike to this popular site offers a stunning panorama toward Mount San Antonio. The trail's proximity to ski resorts, such as Mountain High and Mount Baldy, make it ideal for tackling several sports in one region.

From Lone Pine Canyon Road, the route climbs for 3 miles along Lytle Creek Road, which in winter is snow-covered and passable only by foot. At the top of the ridge, the road intersects the PCT, which splits toward Gobblers Knob, a half-mile northwest. Gaining more than 500 feet from the PCT to the summit, the trail rewards hikers with breathtaking views from the turnaround point at Gobblers Knob.

Once known for the turkeys that roamed here, Gobblers Knob was named by a U.S. Forest Service officer. Today, the prominence is famous for its spectacular views of Stockton Flat and Telegraph Peak.

| Approaching the PCT from Lytle Creek Road

In Detail

Begin where Lone Pine Canyon Road meets Lytle Creek Road. In summer, you can actually drive up Lytle Creek Road to the PCT trailhead. But the 7-mile round-trip excursion described here is a winter trek that requires parking outside the gate at Lytle Creek Road and hiking 3 miles up to the PCT.

From the bottom of this dirt road, begin heading west toward the ridge where the PCT runs north to south. The route passes several farmhouses—including Clyde Ranch, named for pioneer rancher Almon Clyde.

The relentless ascent bends after 1 mile, only to switch back again at 2 miles. To the east are beautiful views of Circle Mountain Ridge, which lies just beyond Lone Pine Canyon Road.

Now paralleling the PCT, the dirt road actually overshoots Gobblers Knob in the distance before making one final switchback. Continue on the route up to the ridge-

line, and keep following Lytle Creek Road to its termination point. This location, which serves as a PCT parking area and entry point, can be accessed by car when roads are clear of snow. Because hikers can drive to this point near the base of the summit for much of the year, it is even more rewarding and appealing to make the route a wintertime snowshoe experience.

Now beyond 6,000 feet, pass the parking area and follow the PCT northwest, climbing along the slope. Continue half a mile to Gobblers Knob. Dotted with Christmas-berry shrubs, this area has space for overnight camping if you want to linger. Expect to have visitors, however, as this area is extremely popular with seasonal hunters.

From Gobblers Knob, head back in the direction from which you came. Enjoy an easy descent along the PCT, and then retrace your steps down Lytle Creek Road to Lone Pine Canyon Road.

Hike 42

Grassy Hollow to Inspiration Point

Distance: 2 miles round-trip

Hiking time: 1 hour

Trail highlights: Mountain views, proximity to ski areas

Difficulty: ▲

Family friendly: ▲▲▲▲▲

Scenery: ▲▲▲

Solitude: ▲

Trail condition: ▲▲▲▲

Getting There

From the town of Wrightwood, take Highway 2 west past the Mountain High Ski Resort. Stay on Highway 2 (Angeles Crest Highway), past the Big Pines junction, and take it to the Grassy Hollow Visitor Center. The Center is located about 6 miles west of Wrightwood and 2.6 miles west of Big Pines junction. To reach the PCT, walk across the Grassy Hollow parking lot, just opposite the restrooms. All vehicles must display a Forest Adventure Pass, available for $5 per day from the Grassy Hollow Visitor Center.

GPS TRAILHEAD COORDINATES

UTM Zone	11S
Easting	433631
Northing	3804048
Latitude	N34.37568°
Longitude	W117.72187°

Overview

This stretch of the Angeles National Forest is an ideal place to introduce hiking to children. Although this family-friendly hike is brief, it does not disappoint when it comes to the view. Beginning from the Grassy Hollow Visitor Center, the trail follows the PCT south toward Blue Ridge. Several switchbacks give way to intermittent mountain vistas, but it's the midway point that will blow your mind.

Resting on the saddle of Blue Ridge, the famed landmark known as "Inspiration Point," offers views of Pine Mountain, Iron Mountain, Mount Baden Powell, and Mount Baldy—the highest peak in the San Gabriel Mountains. Wooden benches overlooking the range make this a good spot to enjoy lunch with a view.

In Detail

The trail begins at the Grassy Hollow Visitor Center, opened in 1996 after the neighboring visitor center in Big Pines was destroyed by arson a decade earlier. In 1997, a wildfire burned 18,000 acres around Grassy Hollow, but fortunately the immediate area around the center was spared. Today it serves as a resource center with nature exhibits and interpretive programs for children.

Begin at the PCT post across from the restrooms and head south (right) on the trail. A massive fallen tree cuts across the center of the path, serving as the gateway

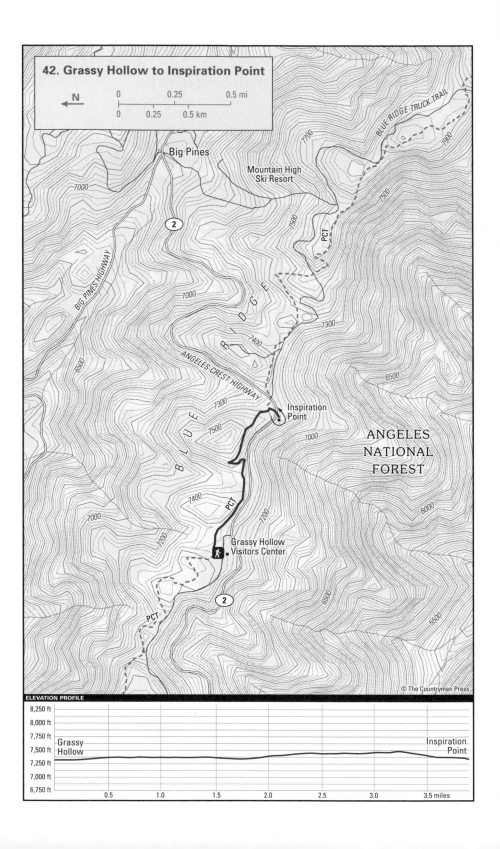

42. Grassy Hollow to Inspiration Point

N

| 0 | 0.25 | 0.5 mi |
| 0 | 0.25 | 0.5 km |

Big Pines

Mountain High
Ski Resort

BLUE RIDGE TRUCK TRAIL

7700

7900

7000

2

BIG PINES HIGHWAY

7500

7500

PCT

6500

7000

7000

7400

7300

ANGELES CREST HIGHWAY

B L U E   R I D G E

7300

Inspiration
Point

7500

7000

ANGELES
NATIONAL
FOREST

6500

7400

PCT

7200

6000

7000

7200

Grassy Hollow
Visitors Center

2

6500

6000

PCT

5500

© The Countryman Press

ELEVATION PROFILE

8,250 ft							
8,000 ft							
7,750 ft	Grassy						Inspiration
7,500 ft	Hollow						Point
7,250 ft							
7,000 ft							
6,750 ft							

0.5   1.0   1.5   2.0   2.5   3.0   3.5 miles

| View from Inspiration Point

to the route. In winter, families use the slope left of the PCT as a sledding area.

To your right, Highway 2 parallels the trail, making this section something of an eyesore. At half a mile, the PCT will slightly climb two switchbacks. At the second curve, be sure to stay to your right since the spur trail to your left heads to Lighting Ridge Nature Trail.

As you near 1 mile, a wooden bench is perched near an outcrop of rocks to the right. This point marks a descent to the Blue Ridge parking lot and restrooms. From here, leave the PCT and cross over Highway 2 toward Inspiration Point at 7,381 feet.

Overlooking the East Fork of the San Gabriel River Basin, Inspiration Point has a direction finder that labels most major peaks in the area. Among them are Pine Mountain, Mount Baldy, Iron Mountain, and Mount Baden Powell, named after Boy Scouts Founder, Baden Powell. At an elevation of 10,064 feet, the mighty Mount Baldy (a.k.a. Mount San Antonio) is the highest peak in the San Gabriel Mountains and the tallest point in Los Angeles County. From Inspiration Point you can see all the way to Santa Catalina Island on clear days.

To complete the hike, cross back over Highway 2 and head northbound on the PCT to Grassy Hollow Visitor Center, where the route began. The visitor center is open Saturdays and Sundays from 10 A.M. to 4 P.M. For more information, call 626-821-6737.

43. Grassy Hollow to Vincent Gap

N

| 0 | 0.25 | 0.5 mi |
| 0 | 0.25 | 0.5 km |

7300
7500
7000
Inspiration
Point
PCT
7400
7200
7000
7200
Grassy Hollow
Visitors Center
2
BIG PINES HIGHWAY
6000
6500
6300
Jackson
Lake
ANGELES
NATIONAL
FOREST
BLUE RIDGE
PCT
7500
Jackson Flat
7200
7000
7300
7500
ANGELES CREST HIGHWAY
6700
6500
6000
6500
7000
6500
6300
7000
7500
PINYON RIDGE TRUCK TRAIL
7000
Vincent Gap
6500
BIG ROCK CREEK RD
2
PCT
7500

© The Countryman Press

ELEVATION PROFILE

| 7,750 ft |
| 7,500 ft |
| 7,250 ft |
| 7,000 ft |
| 6,750 ft |
| 6,500 ft |
| 6,250 ft |

Grassy
Hollow

Vincent
Gap

1.0   2.0   3.0 miles

Hike 43

Grassy Hollow to Vincent Gap

Distance: 7 miles round-trip or 3.5 miles with shuttle
Hiking time: 4 hours
Trail highlights: Mountain views, nearby camping at Jackson Flat, forest trail
Difficulty: ▲▲▲
Family friendly: ▲
Scenery: ▲▲
Solitude: ▲▲▲
Trail condition: ▲▲▲

Getting There

From the town of Wrightwood, take Highway 2 west past the Mountain High Ski Resort. Stay on Highway 2 (Angeles Crest Highway), past Big Pines junction, until you reach the Grassy Hollow Visitor Center. The Center is located about 6 miles west of Wrightwood and 2.6 miles west of Big Pines junction. To reach the PCT, walk across the Grassy Hollow parking lot, just opposite the restrooms.

One-way hikers who plan on shuttling

| Heading north toward Vincent Gap

back from Vincent Gap can leave a second car at the large parking area at mile marker 74.8. It is located on Highway 2, past Grassy Hollow, at the bottom of the canyon. In winter, this parking area can only be accessed by way of Wrightwood, since the pass is often closed.

All vehicles must display a Forest Adventure Pass, available for $5 per day. Passes can be purchased at the Grassy Hollow Visitor Center, open Saturday and Sunday from 10 A.M. to 4 P.M. For more information, call 626-821-6737.

GPS TRAILHEAD COORDINATES

UTM Zone	11S
Easting	433631
Northing	3804048
Latitude	N34.37568°
Longitude	W117.72187°

Overview

This trail begins just past the Mountain High Ski Resort, allowing for winter hikers to experience multiple outdoors sports within close proximity. Launching from the Grassy Hollow Visitor Center, the PCT heads north to Vincent Gap and south to Inspiration Point (see Hike 42).

More experienced hikers will enjoy the 7-mile (round-trip) trek to Vincent Gap. Passing through forest terrain, the trail skirts Jackson Flats Campground and eventually spills onto Highway 2. This turnaround point is where the PCT begins the ascent to Mount Baden Powell, a highlight for many PCT thru-hikers. Unless you plan on shuttling back to Grassy Hollow from Vincent Gap, this midway point marks a horrendous climb southbound, with tight switchbacks interspersed along the way. For those able to arrange transportation for a one-way hike, it

| Sweeping views of the Mojave Desert

is recommended to begin at Grassy Hollow and end at Vincent Gap due to the elevation gain on the return leg.

In Detail

Pace yourself on this hike and bring plenty of water since it takes some time to acclimate to the altitude. Remember that during the return route you'll be gaining over 1,000 feet in elevation.

Begin on the northbound PCT at Grassy Hollow Visitor Center, where water, restrooms, and picnic facilities are available. Marking the trailhead is a wooden sign engraved with the PCT distances of 2,277 miles to Canada and 373 miles to Mexico.

Head left, which is the northbound route on the PCT, although most of this stretch actually jogs west.

Follow the well-marked trail as it winds through dense forest toward a service road. Turn right onto the road, and follow it 100 yards until you reconnect with the narrow PCT, giving way to sweeping views of the Mojave Desert. Near the 2-mile point, a spur trail to the right leads to Jackson Lake, 2.5 miles from the PCT. To the immediate left of the spur trail is a ridge that offers mountain views near Jackson Flat Campground.

Pass the Jackson Lake sign, and continue on the PCT as it crosses a fire road and descends all the way to Highway 2.

Tight switchbacks enter an oak forest and then spill onto the paved parking area at Vincent Gulch Divide. This midway point leads to several routes, including Big Rock Campground and Mount Baden Powell at 9,400 feet. Many Los Angeles day-trippers drive to Vincent Gap just to admire the views of Pine Mountain, Mount Baldy, and Vincent Gulch.

Vincent Gap—named for Big Horn Mine founder, Charles Vincent Dougherty—is the turnaround point for this hike. It is more commonly known as the launching point to Mount Baden Powell, located 4 miles away. From here, hike back in the direction from which you came, or shuttle by car to Grassy Hollow via Highway 2.

N

| 0 | | 0.5 | | 1 mi |
| 0 | 0.5 | | 1 km | |

2300

PCT
Monument

Santa Clara River

SOLEDAD

KOA

CANYON RD

FRYER CANYON

2400

2500

2800

INDIAN CANYON RD

2700

3000

3000

MATTOX CANYON

3500

ANGELES
NATIONAL
FOREST

2500

2800

3000

4000

3500

3000

4000

SANTA CLARA DIVIDE RD

4500

4900

4500

4000

North Fork
Ranger Station

North Fork
Saddle

4000

© The Countryman Press

ELEVATION PROFILE

4,000 ft

North Fork
Ranger Station

3,500 ft

3,000 ft

Soledad
Canyon
Rd

2,500 ft

2,000 ft

1.0   2.0   3.0   4.0   5.0   6.0   7.0 miles

Hike 44

Indian Canyon to North Fork Saddle

Distance: 15 miles round-trip	
Hiking time: 7 hours	
Trail highlights: Deep canyons, secluded camping near Mattox Canyon Creek	
Difficulty: ▲▲▲	
Family friendly: ▲	
Scenery: ▲▲	
Solitude: ▲▲▲	
Trail condition: ▲▲▲	

GPS TRAILHEAD COORDINATES

UTM Zone	11S
Easting	383012
Northing	3811329
Latitude	N34.43684°
Longitude	W118.27334°

Getting There

From Los Angeles, head north on Interstate 5. Take State Highway 14 north toward Lancaster/Palmdale. Continue 10 miles on Highway 14 until you reach Exit 11, for Soledad Canyon Road. Turn right onto Soledad Canyon Road, and drive 7.5 miles to the trailhead for Indian Canyon Trail. Parking and restrooms are available at the trailhead, also marked by a PCT post.

In addition to overnighting at Mattox Canyon Creek, camping is available nearby at 7601 Soledad Canyon Road at the Acton/Los Angeles KOA Campground. Rates include pool access, wireless Internet, bathrooms, and drinking water. For reservations, call 661-268-1214.

Overview

Diverse terrain greets hikers on this Angeles National Forest trail, and thanks to low elevations, it can be completed year-round without having to battle snow. Located 45 miles from central Los Angeles, here you will find open chaparral valleys, the lush setting of Mattox Canyon Creek, and views of jagged red rocks and forested mountains.

The smooth, red bark of manzanita trees adds to the scenic blend. Mossy borders help define the easy-to-follow trail through a shaded section. In spring, fiddleneck and yerba santa sprinkle hints of purple and blue trailside. A southeast climb traverses dry, white slopes of crushed granite rock.

In vivid contrast to the paleness of that terrain are the barren trees blackened from the 2008 Angeles Forest fire. It may take decades before the area can fully recover. A highlight of this hike is the beauty found in the depths of Mattox Canyon.

The local area encompasses history as well: A stone monument marks the official completion of the original PCT's construction.

In Detail

Hikers can begin on the north side of Soledad Canyon Road, near the stone monument commemorating the PCT's completion. In 1993, then–Secretary of the Interior, Bruce Babbitt, presented the three-foot-high structure and said, "The trails connect not just land and ecosystems, but [also] people."

From Soledad Canyon Road, walk 100 feet south on Indian Canyon Road, a Forest Service dirt road leading to the Indian Canyon trailhead parking area, on the right. From here, a post marks the southbound trail that follows the PCT into the mouth of Indian Canyon.

The ascending trail briefly parallels Soledad Canyon Road before bending south. Mugwort, yucca, and other desert plants line this sandy stretch. Mountain-lion tracks and the occasional roar resounding over the valleys attest to the presence of wildlife.

Half a mile into the hike, the sight of Soledad Canyon Road fades to the north. Now entering Indian Canyon, the PCT meanders through a chaparral valley parallel to Indian Canyon Road (accessible only by four-wheel-drive vehicles). Cross over the dirt road, and continue on the well-defined PCT. After a short climb, the trail drops into the heart of Indian Canyon. In this remote area, the only sound interrupting the rhythm of nature is the periodic whistle of a distant train.

After reaching the base of Indian Canyon, follow a switchback leading to a small ridge overlooking east-facing Fryer Canyon. Just after 2 miles, the PCT veers east of Indian Canyon Road to take on a new backdrop of rose-colored cliffs.

The trail then departs from chaparral slopes to enter a more-barren landscape charred by fire's wrath. Follow the trail beyond tight switchbacks, where hints of new growth appear. Here, powdery slopes of

| Rippling Indian Canyon

crushed feldspar granite contrast with the jagged red rocks in the distance.

Cross over a series of washes, and continue on the narrow PCT, which traverses high above a ravine. Just before reaching Mattox Canyon, the trail descends toward an emerald flat—the lush valley that lines Mattox Canyon Creek. Sycamores shade this small stream, which flows through May, making it one of the most appealing camping spots in the area. Cross the creek to climb the steep switchbacks that lead out of the valley and into the heart of Mattox Canyon.

Just beyond a PCT post, the trail zig-

Vehicles with four-wheel drive can access this road, which connects with Indian Canyon Road for an 11-mile route back to Indian Canyon trailhead.

At 4,200 feet, the turnaround point at North Fork Saddle tends to be very windy and cold, especially during winter months. Although camping is prohibited at the North Fork Saddle Ranger Station, you may pitch a tent along the PCT near the station if you are overnighting. The station's restrooms, drinking water, and picnic area are available for campers and day-trippers.

From this turnaround point, head 7.5 miles back in the direction from which you came. You will welcome the mostly downhill return to Indian Canyon trailhead and Soledad Canyon Road.

| A cairn marks the way

zags to the top of a firebreak ridge. Just past 5 miles are striking views of the egg carton–like valley of Mill Canyon. Continue past a pile of cairns along one of the steepest sections of the hike. Now gaining serious elevation, you will climb out of the canyon toward the North Fork Saddle Ranger Station.

Near 6 miles, chaparral slopes fade into a dense forest of pine and fir trees. After several switchbacks, the trail drops, crosses a wash, and climbs toward a picnic area at the North Fork Saddle—your destination. You will see the Santa Clara Divide Road (3N17), which cuts east–west of the saddle.

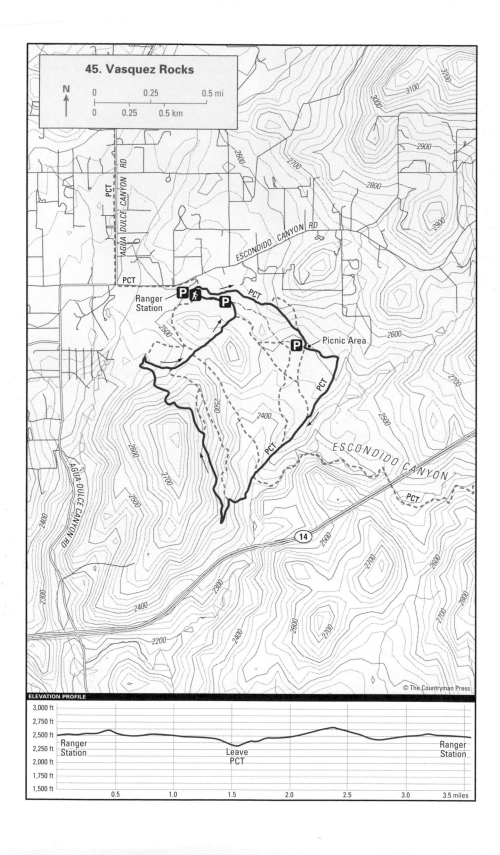

45. Vasquez Rocks

N

| 0 | 0.25 | 0.5 mi |
| 0 | 0.25 | 0.5 km |

AGUA DULCE CANYON RD

PCT

ESCONDIDO CANYON RD

PCT

PCT

Ranger
Station

P

P

Picnic Area

P

2500

2500

2400

2600

2700

2500

PCT

PCT

PCT

ESCONDIDO CANYON

PCT

14

2500

2300

2400

2200

2600

2700

2800

2600

2700

3100

3200

3000

2900

2900

2800

2700

2600

© The Countryman Press

ELEVATION PROFILE

3,000 ft								
2,750 ft								
2,500 ft								
2,250 ft	Ranger			Leave				Ranger
2,000 ft	Station			PCT				Station
1,750 ft								
1,500 ft								

0.5   1.0   1.5   2.0   2.5   3.0   3.5 miles

Hike 45

Vasquez Rocks

Distance: 4-mile loop

Hiking time: 2 hours

Trail highlights: Boulder outcrops

Difficulty: ▲▲

Family friendly: ▲▲▲▲

Scenery: ▲▲▲

Solitude: ▲

Trail condition: ▲▲

Getting There

From Los Angeles, take Highway 5 north to CA 14 (Antelope Valley Freeway). Exit Agua Dulce Canyon Road (exit 15), and head north, following the signs to Vasquez Rocks. Agua Dulce Canyon Road becomes Escondido Canyon Road. The park entrance is on the right. Pass the small ranger station, and either park in the first lot beyond the gates or continue to the larger parking area near the rocks. There are no parking fees or permits required for this area. Park gates are open daily from 8 A.M. to 5 P.M..

GPS TRAILHEAD COORDINATES

UTM Zone	11S
Easting	378751
Northing	3817127
Latitude	N34.48862°
Longitude	W118.32053°

Overview

Setting this hike apart from other sections along the PCT are the distinct sandstone rocks molded into surreal formations. Dramatically tilted into jagged shapes, these rocks gain their form from the action of the San Andreas Fault. The route is relatively easy to follow by way of the PCT, but once it enters the rock canyon, it becomes a labyrinth of routes. Fortunately, the county park encompasses only 902 acres, which means that "getting lost" will probably take you from a faint trail back to a marked one, eventually looping back to the trailhead. Allow extra time to explore various spur trails, and avoid hiking between May and September, when the area is unbearably hot.

In Detail

If you were able to get a parking spot near the ranger station, begin by hiking along the Geology Trail. This child-friendly section has plants and rocks labeled along the way, as well as information about the area's earthquake geology. Otherwise, you can pick up the PCT behind the rocks at the second parking area. For those who started on the Geology Trail, head south on the PCT toward the tilted rock slabs, some jutting at 50 degree angles. This mound brings you head-on with the park's largest rock formations, some up to 150 feet.

Pass the large parking area toward your

right, where junipers, yucca, and chamise grow nearby. The PCT skirts around the back of Vasquez Rocks, where msny day visitors come to scramble up this most prominent section of the park. A wide clearing, dotted with picnic tables, is where the larger parking area meets the PCT. You can begin here if you parked in this second lot.

Continue on the PCT past pepper trees, matchweed, and hollyleaf cherry shrubs. The trail bends south, now with the rocks to your right and the highway to your left. As you soak in the views, you'll notice that the crowds begin to thin along this ridge. Near 1.5 miles, the PCT widens before dropping into Escondido Canyon. A post here marks where the July 2007 wildfire took place.

Beavertail cactus and Mormon tea shrubs grow trailside. At 1.5 miles, the trail splits left to continue southbound on the PCT and right to the horse-and-foot trail. Leave the PCT and head right. Avoid taking any spur trails and animal paths that branch off the main route. Pass the horse trail to the right, and continue straight on the foot trail.

Just before 2 miles, a post labeled "Foot Trail—Stay on the Trail" will mark your right turn into the heart of the rock valley. Leave behind any view of Highway 14, and set your eyes on the massive sandstone boulders, a hideout for the California bandit Tiburcio Vasquez in 1873.

Meandering past gorges, ridges, and cliffs, the Foot Trail passes multiple spur trails to the right, all of which eventually lead back to the parking area. Although it seems difficult at times, stay on the main Foot Trail by following the posts labeled with yellow writing. This area is not well marked, especially toward the center of the valley.

At 2.5 miles, drop north along the Foot Trail, which winds its way back to the parking area. This network of trails can get confusing, but if you head north toward the prominent Vasquez Rocks, you will eventually loop back to the parking area.

| Vasquez Rocks in the distance

Appendix A: Recommended Hikes

Best Scenery

4 Morena Butte
7 Boulder Oaks to Kitchen Creek Falls
15 Big Laguna Trail Loop
17 Garnet Peak
30 Spitler Peak Trail to Tahquitz Valley
37 Cougar Crest Trail to Bertha Peak
39 Splinters Cabin to Upper Deep Creek
45 Vasquez Rocks

Most Difficult

2 Hauser Canyon to CA 94
3 Lake Morena to Hauser Canyon
22 Oriflamme–Rodriguez Loop
24 Scissors Crossing to CA 78/Banner
25 Scissors Crossing to Barrel Springs
29 Fobes Trail to Spitler Peak Trail
30 Spitler Peak Trail to Tahquitz Valley
44 Indian Canyon to North Fork Saddle

Steepest

25 Scissors Crossing to Barrel Springs
37 Cougar Crest Trail to Bertha Peak
43 Grassy Hollow to Vincent Gap
44 Indian Canyon to North Fork Saddle

Easiest

1 CA 94 to Mexican Border
5 Buckman Springs to Lake Morena
11 Desert View Trail
13 Foster Point
18 Pioneer Mail to Kwaaymii Point

Best for Isolation

2 Hauser Canyon to CA 94
3 Lake Morena to Hauser Canyon
16 Indian Creek Loop
21 Mason Valley Truck Trail–PCT Loop
22 Oriflamme–Rodriguez Loop
27 Agua Caliente Creek
39 Splinters Cabin to Upper Deep Creek

Best for Children

5 Buckman Springs to Lake Morena
9 Cottonwood Creek Falls
11 Desert View Trail
12 Monument Peak
13 Foster Point
18 Kwaaymii Point to Pioneer Mail
42 Grassy Hollow to Inspiration Point
45 Vasquez Rocks

Wildflower Hikes

4 Morena Butte
15 Big Laguna Trail Loop
20 Sunrise Highway to Lake Cuyamaca
26 Barrel Springs to Warner Springs
30 Spitler Peak to Tahquitz Valley

Wildlife Hikes

35 Cottonwood to Whitewater Canyon
36 Whitewater Canyon Preserve to Mission Creek Preserve
39 Splinters Cabin to Upper Deep Creek

Appendix B: Outdoors Shops in Southern California

Adventure 16

www.adventure16.com

▲ 2002 South Coast Highway
Oceanside, CA 92054
760-966-1700

▲ 4620 Alvarado Canyon Road
San Diego, CA 92120
619-283-2374

▲ 143 South Cedros Avenue
Solana Beach, CA 92075
858-755-7662

▲ 5425 Reseda Boulevard
Tarzana, CA 91356
818-345-4266

▲ 11161 West Pico Boulevard
Los Angeles, CA 90064
310-473-4574

Bargain Center Surplus

▲ 3015 North Park Way
San Diego, CA 92104
619-295-1181

Big 5 Sporting Goods

www.big5sportinggoods.com

▲ 1253 East Valley Parkway
Escondido, CA 92027
760-480-6860

▲ 949 Lomas Santa Fe Drive
Solana Beach, CA 92075
858-755-5953

▲ 8145 Mira Mesa Boulevard
San Diego, CA 92126
858-693-4941

▲ 16773-B Bernardo Center Drive
Rancho Bernardo, CA 92128
858-673-9219

▲ 4348 Convoy Street
San Diego, CA 92111
858-560-0311

▲ 666 Fletcher Parkway
San Diego, CA 92120
619-444-8139

▲ 3729 Rosecrans Street
San Diego, CA 92110
619-298-3350

▲ 760 Sycamore Avenue
Vista, CA 92083
760-727-2859

▲ 6061-A El Cajon Boulevard
San Diego, CA 92115
619-583-7930

▲ 2301 Vista Way
Oceanside, CA 92054
760-757-4154
858-483-8100

GI Joes Army & Navy

▲ 799 El Cajon Boulevard
El Cajon, CA 92020
619-531-1910

REI

www.rei.com

▲ 2015 Birch Road, Suite 150
Chula Vista, CA 91915
619-591-4924

▲ 1590 Leucadia Boulevard
Encinitas, CA 92024
760-944-9020

▲ 5556 Copley Drive
San Diego, CA 92111
858-279-4400

Sport Chalet
www.sportchalet.com

▲ 3695 Midway Drive
San Diego, CA 92110
619-224-6777

▲ 1640 Camino Del Rio North
San Diego, CA 92108
619-718-7070

▲ 4545 La Jolla Village Drive
San Diego, CA 92122
858-453-5656

▲ 177 South Las Posas Drive
San Marcos, CA 92078
760-744-1804

▲ 27551 Puerta Real
Mission Viejo, CA 92691
949-582-3363

▲ 25560 The Old Road
Valencia, CA 91381
661-253-3883

Sports Authority
www.sportsauthority.com

▲ 5500 Grossmont Center Drive
La Mesa, CA 91942
619-697-8160

▲ 7725 Balboa Avenue
San Diego, CA 92111
858-292-0800

▲ 11690 Carmel Mountain Road
San Diego, CA 92128
858-673-9700

▲ 390 East H Street
Chula Vista, CA 91910
619-476-7234

▲ 1050 North El Camino Real
Encinitas, CA 92024
760-634-6690

▲ 1352 West Valley Parkway
Escondido, CA 92029
760-735-8501

▲ 2160 Vista Way
Oceanside, CA 92054
760-967-1891

▲ 8550 Rio San Diego Drive
San Diego, CA 92108
619-295-1682

| Wildflowers near Lake Cuyamaca

Appendix C: Purchasing Maps and Adventure Passes

National Forest Adventure Pass
Pass Program Headquarters–Pass Orders
602 South Tippecanoe Avenue
San Bernardino, CA 92408-2607
909-382-2621/2622/2623
www.fs.fed.us
www.mountaininfo.com

Adventure 16
www.adventure16.com

Halfmile's GPS Waypoints and Tracks
www.pctmap.net

National Forest Store
406-329-3024
fs_national_forest_store@fs.fed.us

REI
www.rei.com

San Gorgonio Wilderness Association
www.sgwa.org/store.htm

U.S. Geological Survey
www.usgs.gov/pubprod

Appendix D: Hiking Clubs and Organizations

**Back Country Land Trust
of San Diego County**
338 West Lexington Avenue, Suite 204
El Cajon, CA 92020
www.bclt.org

Encinitas Trails Coalition
330 Rosemary Lane
Olivenhain, CA 92024
www.trails4encinitas.org

Fallbrook Land Conservancy
P.O. Box 2701
Fallbrook, CA 92028-2701
760-728-0889
www.fallbrooklandconservancy.org

San Elijo Lagoon Conservancy
P.O. Box 230634
Encinitas, CA 92023
760-436-3944
www.sanelijo.org

Sierra Club, San Diego Chapter
8304 Clairmont Mesa Boulevard
San Diego, CA 92111
858-569-6005
www.sandiego.sierraclub.org

Walkabout International
2650 Truxtun Road
San Diego, CA 92106
619-231-7463
www.walkabout-int.org

Appendix E: Equipment Checklist

Backpack
Bandana
Batteries
Binoculars
Camera and/or journal
Camping soap
Cell phone
Compass
Cooking pots/pans
Duct tape
Eating utensils
First-aid kit (see "Safety"
    section for detailed
    supply list)
Flashlight
Food
Gloves
GPS unit

Hat
Hiking shoes
Identification
Keys
Lip balm
Maps
Matches/lighter
Mosquito repellent
Pants
Pepper spray
Pocketknife
Raincoat
Rope
Sewing kit
Shorts
Sleeping bag and
    sleeping mattress
Small towel

Socks (wool or
    polypropylene)
Sponge
Stove
Sunblock
Sunglasses
Tent
Toilet paper and plastic bag
Toothbrush and toothpaste
T-shirts
Watch
Water bottle(s)
Water filter or purification
    tablets
Whistle
Wilderness Visitor Permit
Windbreaker

| PCT paralleling rock wall near Tahquitz Creek

Appendix F: Web Resources

American Hiking Society
www.americanhiking.org

American Trails
www.americantrails.org

America Walks
www.americawalks.org

Forest Service Volunteer Association
www.fsva.org

Pacific Crest Trail Association
www.pcta.org

San Bernardino National Forest
www.fs.fed.us/r5/sanbernardino

San Gorgonio Wilderness Association
www.sgwa.org

Sierra Club
www.sierraclub.org/ca

Smokey Bear
www.smokeybear.com

Trails.com
www.trails.com

United States Forest Service
www.fs.fed.us

The Wildlands Conservancy
www.wildlandsconservancy.org

Appendix G: Conservation Organizations

▲ Mission Creek Preserve
60550 Mission Creek Road
Desert Hot Springs, CA 92240
760-369-7105
www.wildlandsconservancy.org

▲ Sierra Club, San Diego Chapter
8304 Clairmont Mesa Boulevard
San Diego, CA 92111
858-569-6005
www.sandiego.sierraclub.org

▲ Whitewater Canyon Preserve
9160 Whitewater Canyon Road
Whitewater, CA 92282
760-325-7222
www.wildlandsconservancy.org

| Indian paintbrush

Appendix H: Agencies, National and State Park Districts, and Ranger Stations

▲ Angeles National Forest
  Supervisor's Office
701 North Santa Anita Avenue
Arcadia, CA 91006
626-574-5200

▲ Anza-Borrego Desert State Park
200 Palm Canyon Drive
Borrego Springs, CA 92004
760-767-5311

▲ Arrowhead Ranger Station
28104 Highway 18
P.O. Box 350
Skyforest, CA 92385
909-382-2782

▲ Big Bear Ranger Station
  & Discovery Center
40971 North Shore Drive, Highway 38
Fawnskin, CA 92333
909-382-2790

▲ Cleveland National Forest
Descanso & Palomar Ranger Districts
10845 Rancho Bernardo Road, Suite 200
San Diego, CA 92127
Descanso: 858-673-6180
Palomar: 760-788-0250

▲ Idyllwild Ranger Station
54270 Pine Crest
P.O. Box 518
Idyllwild, CA 92549
909-382-2921

▲ Los Angeles River Ranger District
12371 North Little Tujunga Canyon Road
San Fernando, CA 91342
818-899-1900

▲ Lytle Creek Ranger Station
1209 Lytle Creek Road
Lytle Creek, CA 92358
909-382-2851

▲ San Bernardino National Forest
Supervisor's Office
602 South Tippecanoe Avenue
San Bernardino, CA 92408
909-382-2600

▲ Mill Creek Center, San Gorgonio
  Wilderness Association
34701 Mill Creek Road
Mentone, CA 92359
909-382-2882

▲ Santa Clara/Mojave Rivers
  Ranger District
33708 Crown Valley Road
Acton, CA 93510
661-269-2808

▲ Santa Rosa and San Jacinto Mountains
  National Monument Visitors Center
51500 Highway 74
Palm Desert, CA 92260
760-862-9984

▲ Wildlands Conservancy/Mission
  Creek Preserve
60550 Mission Creek Road
Desert Hot Springs, CA 92240
760-369-7105

▲ Wildlands Conservancy/White-
  water Preserve
9150 Whitewater Canyon Road
Whitewater, CA 92282
760-325-7222

Appendix I: Suggested Reading

Belzer, Thomas. *Roadside Plants of Southern California.* Missoula, MT: Mountain Press Publishing Company, 1984.

Berger, Karen, and Smith R. Daniel. *The Pacific Crest Trail: A Hiker's Companion.* Woodstock, VT: Countryman Press, 2014.

Brown, Ann Marie, and Tom Stienstra. *California Hiking: The Complete Guide to More Than 1,000 Hikes.* 7th ed. Emeryville, CA: Avalon Travel Publishing, 2005.

Go, Ben. *Pacific Crest Trail Data Book.* Berkeley: Wilderness Press, 2007.

Jenkins, Ruby, Jeffrey Schaffer, Ben Schifrin, and Thomas Winnett. *Pacific Crest Trail: From the Mexican Border to Tuolumne Meadows.* Berkeley: Wilderness Press, 2007.

Kavanagh, James. *California Trees and Wildflowers: A Pocket Naturalist Guide.* Guilford, CT: Waterford Press, 2000.

Schad, Jerry. *Afoot and Afield in San Diego County.* 4th edition. Berkeley: Wilderness Press, 2007.

Strayed, Cheryl. *Wild: From Lost to Found on the Pacific Crest Trail.* New York: Knopf, 2012.

Weland, Gerald. *A Guide to Locating California Wildflowers.* Phoenix: American Traveler Press, 2007.

| Approaching Vasquez Rocks